Green Line 3

Vorschläge zur Leistungsmessung

von
Pauline Ashworth
Elizabeth Daymond
Elise Köhler-Davidson
Carolyn Jones
Stefan Rauschenberg

herausgegeben von
Harald Weisshaar

Ernst Klett Verlag
Stuttgart · Leipzig

Vorwort

Liebe Lehrerin, lieber Lehrer,

die *Green Line 3 Vorschläge zur Leistungsmessung* orientieren sich an den Anforderungen für die Leistungsfeststellung am Gymnasium. Wie Sie wissen, legen aktuelle Lehrpläne Wert auf Kompetenzorientierung und kommunikativen Anspruch. Darauf haben wir bei der Entwicklung dieses Hefts besonderen Wert gelegt, um Ihnen Aufgaben anzubieten, die auf dem neuesten Stand sind und sich daher optimal für die Erstellung von Klassenarbeiten eignen.

Aufbau

Kompetenzbereiche: Pro Unit werden Materialien für Klassenarbeiten zu *Listening, Reading, Writing, Mediation*, Grammatik und Wortschatz sowie *Speaking* angeboten. Entsprechend den unterschiedlichen Voraussetzungen einiger Bundesländer werden die Aufgaben zur *Grammatik* und zum *Wortschatz* getrennt angeboten. Diese Materialien können somit einfach nach Bedarf eingesetzt werden. Ab S. 55 finden Sie einen *Revision*-Teil mit Aufgabenvorschlägen zu einigen Grammatikpensen aus Green Line 2.
Die Aufgaben sind thematisch nach *Units* gegliedert, und folgen der Progression des Vokabulars im Schülerbuch. Das Symbol ▲ zeigt an, dass es sich bei der gekennzeichneten Aufgabe um eine vergleichsweise anspruchsvolle Aufgabe handelt. Entsprechend der Progression des Schülerbuchs finden Sie nach jeder Unit Aufgabenvorschläge zu den vier *Text smart*-Teilen.

Die beiliegende **CD-ROM** enthält alle Tests und Lösungen als PDF und in editierbarer Form. So können Aufgaben gezielt ausgewählt und die Klassenarbeit individuell zusammengestellt werden. Auf der CD-ROM befinden sich zudem die Audiodateien und Filme (jeweils mit Transkript) zu den Hörverstehen- bzw. Hör- / Sehverstehensaufgaben im Heft. Pro Unit bieten wir Ihnen auf der CD-ROM darüber hinaus einen Vordruck für eine Förderempfehlung an (s. u.).

Die sprachliche Fertigkeit ***Speaking*** kann anhand von drei Schritten getestet werden: *Warm-up* (kurzes L-S Gespräch), *monologue* und *dialogue*. Themenentsprechende *Monologue-* und *Dialogue-Speaking cards* sowie *Teacher's notes* finden Sie im Heft und auf der CD-ROM. Zu manchen Units gibt es zwei *Dialogue-Speaking cards*, die alternativ eingesetzt werden können. Wie die einzelnen *Speaking cards* zu verwenden sind können Sie an der Symbolik auf der Rückseite erkennen.

Materialien zur Förderempfehlung

Binnendifferenzierung und individuelle Förderung sind zentrale Bestandteile eines innovativen Fremdsprachenunterrichts, der die Bedürfnisse der einzelnen Schülerinnen und Schüler in den Mittelpunkt rückt und somit zu einem bestmöglichen individuellen Kompetenzaufbau beiträgt. Diese zentralen Bestandteile werden auch in den vorliegenden *Vorschläge zur Leistungsmessung* aufgegriffen. Auf der beiliegenden CD-ROM finden Sie pro Unit eine Förderempfehlung als PDF (für Unit 1 auf S. 3 auch in gedruckter Form) und auch als Word-Datei (editierbar), die es Ihnen ermöglicht, allen Schülerinnen und Schülern, die Förderbedarf aufweisen, eine gezielte Rückmeldung zu diesem zu geben. Die Förderempfehlungen zeigen auf, was die Schülerinnen und Schüler in welchem Kompetenzbereich konkret aufarbeiten und wiederholen müssen, um ihren Förderbedarf auszugleichen. Darüber hinaus erfolgen ausgewählte Querverweise zu passenden Hilfestellungen (bspw. vertiefendes Übungsmaterial) in das Schülerbuch oder Workbook. Dieses Vorgehen ermöglicht nicht nur den Ausgleich des individuellen Förderbedarfs, sondern dient Ihren Schülerinnen und Schülern, deren Eltern und Ihnen auch als Grundlage der Dokumentation des Kompetenzaufbaus und der frühzeitigen Beseitigung von Lernhindernissen. Auf diese Weise erwerben Ihre Schülerinnen und Schüler auch methodische Kompetenzen, erlernen Techniken selbstständigen und eigenverantwortlichen Lernens und nutzen die Förderempfehlungen als *advance organizers* zur Planung und Steuerung ihrer Lernprozesse.

Kommentar zur individuellen Förderung

Name: **Klasse:**

Förderempfehlung: Diese Dinge haben nicht so gut geklappt:		**Kompetenzbereich**	**Ausgewähltes Material zur Vertiefung und Wiederholung**
☐	Ich muss noch üben, einem Text, den ich höre, Informationen zu entnehmen (Schwerpunkt: Gespräch über Ratschläge / Aushandeln eines Kompromisses).	Hören	**SB:** S. 9/2, S. 16/2; S. 22/1 **WB:** S. 3/3; S. 6/10, S. 15/1
☐	Ich muss noch üben, einem Text, den ich lese, Informationen zu entnehmen (Schwerpunkt: Ratschläge).	Lesen	**SB:** S. 10/1, S. 14/9 **WB:** S. 12/22–23
☐	Ich muss mir noch einmal anschauen und trainieren, wie ich einen Text (E-Mail) verfassen kann, in dem ich Ratschläge erteile.	Schreiben	**SB:** S. 13/8, S. 22/3, S. 26/11 **WB:** S. 8/14, S. 16/3
☐	Ich muss mir noch einmal anschauen und trainieren, wie ich das Ende einer Geschichte schreiben kann.	Schreiben	**SB:** S. 14/9, S. 20/4 **WB:** S. 12/24
☐	Ich muss noch einmal üben und wiederholen, wie ich ein Bild beschreiben und in einem Dialog Ratschläge erteilen / nach Ratschlägen fragen kann	Sprechen	**SB:** S. 8/1, S. 16/3, S. 20/3, S. 21/1 **WB:** S. 5/9, S. 7/13, S. 11/21
☐	Ich muss noch einmal trainieren, wie ich den Inhalt einer deutschsprachigen E-Mail (Bitte um Unterstützung) auf Englisch wiedergeben kann.	Mediation	**SB:** S. 13/6 **WB:** S. 8/15
☐	Ich muss noch einmal trainieren, wie ich den Inhalt einer englischsprachigen Homepage über einen Wettbewerb auf Deutsch wiedergeben kann.	Mediation	**SB:** S. 24/7
☐	Ich muss die Vokabeln aus Unit 1 noch einmal wiederholen: ☐ Wortfeld Interessen und Persönlichkeiten ☐ weiteres Unit-Vokabular	Wortschatz	**SB:** S. 9/3, S. 16/1, S. 23/4, S. 25/9 **WB:** S. 2/1, S. 5/8, S. 7/13
☐	Ich muss die Bedingungssätze Typ 2 wiederholen: ☐ Bildung ☐ Verwendung ☐ Unterscheidung zwischen Typ 1 und Typ 2	Grammatik	**SB:** S. 11/3, S. 12/4–5, S. 27/12 **WB:** S. 3/5, S. 4/6, S. 15/2
☐	Ich muss üben, wie ich Reflexivpronomen und *each other* richtig anwenden kann: ☐ Reflexivpronomen ☐ *each other*	Grammatik	**SB:** S. 15/10–11, S. 24/6 **WB:** S. 6/11, S. 7/12

Weitere Anmerkungen:

Ich habe von der Klassenarbeit meines Sohnes/meiner Tochter und von der Förderempfehlung Kenntnis genommen.

(Unterschrift einer/s Erziehungsberechtigten)

Green Line 3
Vorschläge zur Leistungsmessung
ISBN 978-3-12-834234-4

Inhalt des Hefts

Unit 1 Find your place

1 Listening: I need some advice!

Either:

Listen to Holly and Luke's conversation. Answer the questions in 1-5 words.

1. Why does Holly like quizzes? ______
2. How does Holly know that Luke is competitive? ______
3. What did Holly think of the bracelet Luke made? ______
4. Why does Luke think that he is imaginative? ______
5. How did Luke show his talent for helping people? ______
6. What dream does Holly hope to achieve? ______

Or:

a) *Listen and tick ✓ the correct answer.*	**true**	**false**
1. Luke thinks the quiz is a waste of time.		
2. Holly always believes the results of quizzes.		
3. Holly disagrees that Luke is competitive.		
4. Luke thinks he has a talent for making things.		
5. Luke and Holly disagree that Luke's imagination is good.		
6. Holly has had experience with Luke's teaching skills.		
7. Luke agrees that he has a talent for explaining things.		
8. Holly doesn't know what she would like to be in the future.		

▲ **b)** *Listen again and correct the wrong sentences.*

Klett
Green Line 3
Vorschläge zur Leistungsmessung
ISBN: 978-3-12-834234-4

2 Listening: Can we compromise?

Either:
Listen to the conversation and tick ✓ the correct answer.

1. Jay wants to …
   a) ☐ play football.
   b) ☐ meet Luke on Saturday.
   c) ☐ watch a football match.

2. Jay's mum thinks he should …
   a) ☐ help the family more at home.
   b) ☐ do more school work.
   c) ☐ spend every Saturday at home.

3. Jay wants to see this match because …
   a) ☐ he wasn't able to see the last one.
   b) ☐ he has seen only two matches.
   c) ☐ he knows this is an important game.

4. First, Jay says he can do his homework …
   a) ☐ on Saturday morning.
   b) ☐ on Saturday afternoon.
   c) ☐ on Saturday evening.

5. Jay then offers to do his homework …
   a) ☐ after the match.
   b) ☐ before the match.
   c) ☐ at his uncle's house.

6. They agree that Jay doesn't have to …
   a) ☐ go to his uncle's.
   b) ☐ get up early on Sunday.
   c) ☐ study on Saturday.

Or:
Listen and complete the phone conversation between Jay and Luke. Use 2 or 3 words in each gap.

Luke: Hi Jay. How are things?

Jay: I've just had a really difficult conversation with Mum! I told her I wanted to go to the ________________ with you but she thinks I should ________________ on Saturday because I need to finish my ________________. I told her I can't miss ________________ in one month! But she said we have to visit ________________ in the evening and that ________________ isn't enough time to do all my homework!

Luke: Oh, no! What are you going to do?

Jay: Well, in the end she agreed that I can go but I have to ________________ early on Sunday morning and do ________________!

Green Line 3
Vorschläge zur Leistungsmessung
ISBN: 978-3-12-834234-4

3 Reading: How to be confident

A Don't say negative things to yourself! Would you speak to your best friend like that? No, of course not – so be nice to yourself! Change the way you think and focus on the positive things!

B Focus on what is going well for you. Don't think about problems that *could* happen in the future. Stop and think – what's good about *now*?

C If you think that you have to be perfect in everything, then you'll never have a chance to succeed! Maybe you think: "I won't try for a place in the football team because I'm not good enough." Then it's sure that someone else will get the place!

D When things go wrong, it can make you stronger. Don't say: "I never succeed in this activity." Instead, say: "Today I didn't do well, but now I know how I can improve."

E Tell yourself that everyone is good at different things. Don't feel bad that your friend is a better musician than you, for example. Maybe you're better at art! Now you can both feel proud!

F Don't worry about things you can't change, like how tall you are or your hair colour. Remember, your friends are more interested in your fun and friendly personality!

Either:

a) *Match each section of the magazine article to a heading. There is one heading you don't need.*

1. Live in the present! _____
2. Learn from your mistakes! _____
3. Celebrate your differences! _____
4. Talk to yourself as you talk to others! _____
5. Stay active! _____
6. You don't have to be the best! _____
7. It's about how you are, not how you look! _____

▲ **b)** *Now think of your own title for this text.*

Or:

Which paragraph gives advice for each problem? Write the letters next to the correct numbers.

1. ____ 2. ____ 3. ____ 4. ____ 5. ____ 6. ____

Klett
Green Line 3
Vorschläge zur Leistungsmessung
ISBN: 978-3-12-834234-4

4 Reading: I want to be famous!

Q: Hello! My life's very boring and every day's the same. I want to be famous and have an exciting life! I don't know what my talents are, but I really want to find out. Has anyone got any advice for me? Thanks. Jamie

A: Well, I'm sure you won't be surprised by the first thing I'm going to say – what do you want to be famous for? You could be famous in the worlds of science, technology or writing – some people really want to make a big difference to the world. But that isn't what you mean, is it? You want to be a big star! I'm sure it's cool to be very rich – you can live in a big house and wear beautiful clothes and travel round the world – but being famous isn't a job (I know a lot of people think it is!). To start with, you have to choose something that you are really good at. Is it music, or acting, or sport ...? Then you have to work hard if you want to succeed – harder than you could ever imagine! While your friends are enjoying themselves after school and at weekends, you will have to practise a lot – until you are too tired to stand up! You have to show that you are different from everyone else so that someone notices you and helps you to succeed. And, when you have problems, don't give up! Always remember your dream – and try, try and try again! Good luck! Rebecca

Either:
Read the posts from an internet forum and complete these sentences in one to five words.

1. Jamie wants to be famous because ______________________________.
2. Rebecca thinks that Jamie just wants ______________________________.
3. First, Jamie must decide what ______________________________.
4. He won't have any free time to ______________________________.
5. If Jamie wants to be noticed, he must show that he isn't ______________________.
6. Jamie must never forget ______________________________.

Or:
Complete the table with information from the text.

Reasons why people want to be famous	Advice for people who want to be famous
1. ____________________	4. ____________________
2. ____________________	5. ____________________
3. ____________________	6. ____________________
	7. ____________________
	8. ____________________

Klett
Green Line 3
Vorschläge zur Leistungsmessung
ISBN: 978-3-12-834234-4

5 Writing: Advice please!

You have received this e-mail from your friend Ella.

Hi, I've got a problem – can I ask you for some advice? You know that my sister, Ruby, is really good at hockey? Well, guess what? Her team is in the finals[1] of the hockey competition. The match is on Friday evening and, of course, she wants all her family and friends there. The only problem is that I've got an important tennis match at the same time and I really don't want to miss it – but I don't want Ruby to be upset with me. I was thinking that I could miss the hockey match but get tickets for a concert[2] that she really wants to go to on Saturday, as a surprise. Do you think that's a good compromise? Ella

1 **finals** Finale | 2 **concert** Konzert

Write an e-mail to Ella. Say that you are happy about her sister's success. Tell her if you agree or disagree with her compromise idea, and give reasons. Tell Ella what you would do in her situation.

____

____

____

____

____

____

▲ 6 Writing: The big match

Read the story and write the ending.

Ruby was very tired but very happy. Her hockey team were winning the match 3-2 and she was the star of the team! She could see all her friends and her parents and brother in the crowd and she felt very proud of her talent. But her sister, Ella, wasn't there – where was she? "If she didn't come, there's going to be a *big* fight later!" Ruby thought. She stopped running and looked everywhere in the crowd for her sister … and at that moment a girl from the other team ran past her towards the goal and … Oh no! 3-3 and only three minutes until the end of the match! …

____

____

____

____

____

____

Green Line 3
Vorschläge zur Leistungsmessung
ISBN: 978-3-12-834234-4

7 Mediation: I've had an idea!

You have a friend from England who is very good with children and who is coming to stay with you and your family soon. Your aunt has two children who have started learning English at school and she has sent you this e-mail. Write an e-mail to your friend and explain what your aunt has written.

> Hi! Ich hatte eine Idee: Würde deine Freundin vielleicht gerne für ein oder zwei Stunden am Tag mit meinen Kindern spielen und mit ihnen Englisch sprechen? Ich fände es toll, wenn sie mit ihr üben könnten! Bestimmt kennt sie ein paar lustige Spiele, die sie mit ihnen spielen könnte und bestimmt hätte sie auch viel Spaß dabei! Es wäre auch nicht schlimm, wenn sie nicht jeden Tag Zeit hätte. Und natürlich würde sie für ihre Zeit etwas Taschengeld von mir bekommen. Falls sie vorhat, in Zukunft mit Kindern zu arbeiten, wäre das für sie eine gute Erfahrung. Könntest du fragen, was sie von der Idee hält und mir Bescheid geben? Danke!

Hi! My aunt has had a good idea – she thinks you could ____________________

____

____

____

____

____

8 Mediation: An animal photo competition

You have a friend who takes good photos of animals and nature. You have seen something on an English website about a photo competition and you think your friend should take part. Your friend's English isn't very good. Phone your friend and tell him/her about the competition.

> **Animal photo competition!**
> Have you taken a great photo of an animal this year? We want to see it! Send us your most creative photo of any animal, big or small, and we will choose the best photo of the year!
> Just imagine – if you won first prize, you would have £1,000 to spend on anything you want!
> And if you won second, you could have a new camera to take even better photos!
>
> Send your photo by e-mail before 4th November and write a short description of where and when you took it. And remember – it must be a photo that you took yourself. Good luck!

Hi! ____________________________________

____

____

____

____

Green Line 3
Vorschläge zur Leistungsmessung
ISBN: 978-3-12-834234-4

9 Vocabulary: Adjectives → (after Station 1)

Think of an adjective to describe each of these people. Sometimes there's more than one possible answer.

1. Thousands of people come to my concerts and listen to my music! ____________________
2. I've got so much money, I don't know what to buy next! ____________________
3. I've got a *lot* of work to do. I don't know how I'm going to finish it all. ____________________
4. I don't like working hard. It's more important to relax and have fun! ____________________
5. I'm very good at sport and I know I'll be a successful tennis player one day. ____________________
6. People say my paintings are different and that I have strange and interesting ideas. ____________________
7. I hate losing – even a computer game against my brother! ____________________
8. I get good marks in school because I know a lot. ____________________

10 Vocabulary: Life isn't fair! → (after Station 2)

Complete the text with the correct words or phrases. You don't need all of the words.

enjoy myself | successful | behave | laid-back | in charge | messy | push myself | give up | bossy | the way I am | competitive | in your shoes

I'm really stressed out at the moment because I've got some important exams next week and my parents say I don't ____________________ enough! Yesterday, my Dad said "If I were ____________________, I would study hard now so I could relax and ____________________ later." But he doesn't understand. I need to see my friends a lot – it's just ____________________! I got angry with them last night and started shouting, but my mum just told me that I couldn't go out again this week. When I'm not studying, I have to tidy my ____________________ room! They're so ____________________! They're always telling me what to do! Oh well – they are my parents and they're ____________________ so for now I'll just have to live with their rules and try to ____________________ better. But life will be very different after the exams!

ISBN: 978-3-12-834234-4

11 Language: My dream → (after Station 1)

Holly's friend Zoe has sent her an e-mail. Fill in the correct verb forms to make if-clauses type 2.

Hi, Holly! I just wanted to tell you that I've finally sent off my fashion designs for the competition.

I ______________ (be) so happy if I ______________ (win), but there are a lot of creative designers out there so I'm not feeling very confident. If I ______________ (have) more time, I ______________ (enter) a lot more competitions because I need the practice.

Even if I ______________ (not win) very often, it ______________ (help) me to learn how I can improve. The prize is usually the chance to see your fashion design in a shop. I ______________ (not sleep) for a week if somebody ______________ (buy) a dress that I designed. If that ______________ (happen), I ______________ (be) so excited! Zoe xoxo

12 Language: If things were different … → (after Station 1)

Finish the second sentence (if-clauses type 2) so that it has the same meaning as the first.

1. I'm not in town on Saturday, so I'm not going to enter the swimming competition.

If ______________________________, ____.

2. Anna doesn't like cooking, so she isn't going to make me a birthday cake.

If ______________________________, ____.

3. Tom doesn't enjoy dancing or singing, so he won't take part in the talent show.

If ______________________________, ____.

4. We don't live near a park so we don't play sport very often.

If ______________________________, ____.

5. They don't like to travel, so they won't go to London.

If ______________________________, ____.

6. Ben doesn't have a talent for Maths so he doesn't like Maths lessons.

If ______________________________, ____.

Green Line 3
Vorschläge zur Leistungsmessung
ISBN: 978-3-12-834234-4

13 Language: The talent show → (after Station 1)

The friends are watching a talent show. Use the prompts to complete their conversations. Use if-clauses type 1 or 2.

Jay:	Why can't I dance like him? (1) If / I / dance / like them, / I / leave / school tomorrow!
Shahid:	You don't live in the real world! (2) If / you / not stop / dreaming, / you / fail / your exams!
Luke:	I love his long hair! (3) I / look / cool too / if / my hair / be / longer!
Holly:	My friend Zoe wants to design dresses like that! (4) If / she / know / how to do it, / she / be / a famous designer!
Olivia:	Are they looking for a saxophone player? (5) I / be / happy to join them / if / they /ask / me!
Gwen:	Why are singing lessons so expensive? (6) If / I / can / have singing lessons, I / be able / to enter next year's show!

1. ______________________________

2. ______________________________

3. ______________________________

4. ______________________________

5. ______________________________

6. ______________________________

▲

14 Language: Your own ideas → (after Station 1)

What will / would you do if ...? Use if-clauses type 1 or 2 to write about yourself.

1. have time next weekend: ______________________________
2. can choose a special talent: ______________________________
3. don't have to go to school: ______________________________
4. decide to celebrate my next birthday: ______________________________

Klett
Green Line 3
Vorschläge zur Leistungsmessung
ISBN: 978-3-12-834234-4

15 Language: Let's talk about ourselves! → (after Station 2)

Complete the sentences with the correct reflexive pronouns.

myself | yourself | herself | himself | yourselves | ourselves | themselves

1. Max taught _______________ to play the saxophone. He's very good!
2. We need to make lunch _______________. Mum's going to be late.
3. Can you help me fix my bike? I can't do it _______________.
4. Lucy and Tom – come and sit down and behave _______________!
5. I'll show you how to take a good photo if you can't do it _______________.
6. The boys didn't push _______________ during the football match, so they lost!
7. Anna painted her bedroom _______________. It's cool, isn't it?

16 Language: Saturday sports camp → (after Station 2)

*Put in the correct reflexive pronoun or **each other**. You can use words more than once.*

"Hi everyone. I'm Will and I'm one of the coaches here. Last year, my friend Liam and I noticed that there wasn't a Saturday sports camp in this town, so we started this one _______________. I'm afraid Liam isn't here today, so I'm going to teach all of you _______________. Now, first you need to get to know _______________. Please turn to your left and present _______________ to your partner. Then, the same to your right. Now, look at _______________ very carefully. These are not your friends! You are going to play different sports against _______________ today and you want to win! You will all have to push _______________ very hard and learn what it means to be winners. The group last week said they understood _______________ much better by the end of the day. Now, volleyball first. I want you all to enjoy _______________ but don't forget, you're in it to win it!"

Green Line 3
Vorschläge zur Leistungsmessung
ISBN: 978-3-12-834234-4

Text smart 1: Poems and songs

Another view

by Bernard Young

This place is full of scenery.
There's not a shop in sight.
I need to buy a burger.
There's nothing here I like.

There's nothing here I like.
It's all hills and trees and lakes
and oldies who love hiking.
I need to phone my mates.

I need to phone my mates
and tell them what I'm going through.
I have to trek for hours
just to admire a view.

'Just admire that view,'
is all my dad can say.
He's driving me round the bend.
I've got to get away.

1 Comprehension

a) *Read the poem and match the phrases with the correct meaning.*

1. "This place is full of scenery."
2. "I need to phone my mates."
3. "And tell them what I'm going through."
4. "I need to trek for hours."
5. "Just admire that view."
6. "He's driving me round the bend."
7. "I need noise and traffic."

A He should see how wonderful the nature he sees is.
B He's making him crazy.
C There's beautiful landscape all around him.
D He wants the action and sounds of busy city streets.
E He needs to call to his friends.
F He has to walk a long way.
G He wants to tell his friends what he must do.

1. ____ 2. ____ 3. ____ 4. ____ 5. ____ 6. ____ 7. ____

b) *Read the poem again. Are these statements true or false?*	**true**	**false**
1. The speaker sees a shop but doesn't have money to buy anything.		
2. The speaker would enjoy the trip if a friend was there too.		
3. The speaker thinks hiking is not an activity for young people.		
4. After a long walk there is only nature to look at.		
5. The father is always trying to ask questions about his child's problems.		
6. At the end of the poem the speaker is beginning to calm down.		

2 Structure and meaning

a) *Describe who and where the speaker (= Sprecher) is and explain how he/she feels about the situation.*

b) *Examine the form of the poem:*

– *Analyse the rhyme scheme.*
– *Which words does the speaker repeat and why?*

Klett
Green Line 3
Vorschläge zur Leistungsmessung
ISBN: 978-3-12-834234-4

Textquellen: © Bernard Young, May 15, 2015

Grandpa

by Berlie Doherty

Grandpa's hands are as rough[1] as garden sacks[2]
And as warm as pockets.
His skin[3] is crushed[4] paper round his eyes
Wrapping up their secrets.

1 **rough** rau | 2 **garden sack** Gartensack | 3 **skin** Haut | 4 **crushed** hier: zusammengeknüllt

1 Comprehension

Poems often use metaphors (which use comparisons) or symbols (which use pictures for ideas) to show meanings. Tick ✓ the correct meaning for the metaphors and symbols in this poem.

1. "Grandpa's hands are rough as garden sacks"
   - a) ☐ Grandpa is very strong.
   - b) ☐ Grandpa is old and has lived a long life.
   - c) ☐ Grandpa has a bad character.

2. "And warm as pockets."
   - a) ☐ Grandpa is a warm person you feel comfortable around.
   - b) ☐ The speaker wants warmer clothes.
   - c) ☐ Grandpa's clothes are old.

3. "His skin is crushed paper round his eyes"
   - a) ☐ Grandpa wears strange glasses.
   - b) ☐ Grandpa often keeps his eyes closed.
   - c) ☐ Grandpa's skin shows that he is old.

4. "Wrapping up their secrets."
   - a) ☐ Grandpa hasn't told people all his thoughts and experiences.
   - b) ☐ Grandpa gives people lots of presents.
   - c) ☐ He doesn't always understand things.

2 Structure and meaning

a) *Examine the rhyme scheme of the poem.*

b) *Complete the following sentences:*

1. The language in this poem is ______________________________.
2. The poem makes me feel ______________ because ______________.
3. I'd describe the relationship between the speaker and grandpa as ______________.

▲ **c)** *Write a similar poem about your grandpa or grandma.*

3 Comparing two poems

a) *In what ways are the two poems similar or different? Think about the form, length (= Länge), rhyme scheme and topic.*

b) *Describe how the speakers of the two poems feel about their families.*

Klett
Green Line 3
Vorschläge zur Leistungsmessung
ISBN: 978-3-12-834234-4

Textquellen: From *Walking on Air* by Berlie Doherty, first published by HarperCollins Publishers Ltd, London, © Berlie Doherty 2014

Unit 2 Let's go to Scotland!

1 Listening: Best of friends?

Either:

a) *Listen and tick ✓ the correct answer.*

	true	false
1. Alfie wants Callum to help him with Sofia.		
2. The boys planned to meet Sofia.		
3. The children meet in Castle Street.		
4. Sofia's from Italy		
5. Sofia likes to play hockey and cricket.		
6. Alfie's been playing in a band for a year.		
7. Alfie invites Sofia to a gig on Friday.		
8. Sofia wants to go to the gig on her own.		

▲ **b)** *Listen again and correct the wrong sentences.*

Or:

a) *Listen to the text and try to understand the gist first. Then read these summaries of the conversation and tick ✓ the best summary.*

1. Callum and Alfie like Sofia, but Sophia likes Alfie. At the end she says she will go to a gig with Alfie and not to the shinty club with Callum. ☐	2. Sofia likes both Callum and Alfie, so she says she will play shinty with Callum and watch Alfie's band with her brother, Jack. ☐
3. Callum and Alfie both want Sofia to be their girlfriend. At the end they find out that she is interested in another boy, Jack. ☐	4. Callum and Alfie both want Sofia to be interested in them, but she doesn't like Callum or Alfie. ☐

b) *Listen again and match the notes to the people. Write the numbers next to the right person or people.*

Sofia:	**Callum:**
Sofia's mum:	**Alfie:**

1. likes Scotland | 2. isn't into sports | 3. has a gig on Friday | 4. likes Italy | 5. plays shinty | 6. does sport | 7. likes Sofia | 8. is from London | 9. goes to school with Alfie | 10. likes Jack

Klett
Green Line 3
Vorschläge zur Leistungsmessung
ISBN: 978-3-12-834234-4

2 Listening: It always rains …

Either:
Listen to the conversation and tick ✓ the correct answer(s). More than one answer can be correct.

1. Where does Grace live?
   a) ☐ Scotland
   b) ☐ England
   c) ☐ Germany

2. What has the weather been like since Emily arrived there?
   a) ☐ It has rained.
   b) ☐ It has been very cold.
   c) ☐ It has been sunny.

3. What does Emily say German people think about the English?
   a) ☐ They're funny.
   b) ☐ They always talk about the weather.
   c) ☐ They don't mind waiting in queues.

4. What does Grace say British people think about the Germans?
   a) ☐ They work a lot.
   b) ☐ They love to laugh at the English.
   c) ☐ They are never late.

5. What does Grace say English people think about the Scots?
   a) ☐ They drink whisky.
   b) ☐ They like to keep their money.
   c) ☐ They eat haggis.

6. What does Grace's dad do now?
   a) ☐ He works in television.
   b) ☐ He speaks Gaelic.
   c) ☐ He works in Scotland.

Or:
Listen to the conversation and make notes about the clichés (= Klischees) for the English, Germans and Scottish.

Country	Cliché
Germany	1. Germans don't have ______
	2. Germans ______
	3. Girls are ______
	4. Germans ______
England	5. The weather ______
	6. The English ______
	7. The English ______
Scotland	8. Scottish people ______
	9. The Scots ______
	10. Scottish people ______

Klett
Green Line 3
Vorschläge zur Leistungsmessung
ISBN: 978-3-12-834234-4

3 Reading: Scotland's islands

Isle of Skye[1] Beautiful, historical, magical! Visit the Isle of Skye for a week and lose your heart forever. Cross the Skye Bridge to get to the island, where you'll see the famous Cuillin[2] Hills. Spend some time here and enjoy their beauty and spectacular views of the island, its countryside and its wildlife. Skye is a great place for birdwatching. People have been living on the island for thousands of years and you can see signs of Skye's past everywhere around you; from dinosaur footprints[3] to Stone Age stone circles to castles of more modern times. When you come to Skye, you discover the real Scotland. Of the 9,000 people who live on Skye now, about 3,000 speak Gaelic. Find out more about the Gaelic culture at the Aros Centre in Portree[4], Skye's biggest town.	**Orkney**[5] Not one but 70 beautiful islands! Nature, food, art, music and, of course, a friendly welcome are just some of the reasons people have been coming to Orkney for thousands of years. Of course, not all of those who came were welcome! If it's history you are interested in, Orkney is the place to visit. Some of the most important Stone Age villages in the whole of Europe are here on Orkney. Visit Skara Brae[6] to see how Stone Age man lived. Orkney is the island for outdoor people. The cliffs, hills and coastline are spectacular and the wildlife is fascinating. If you visit in June or July, you will have time to enjoy everything about the islands as the days are so long and it never really gets dark. Come and enjoy the history and the magical atmosphere of these beautiful islands.

1 **Isle of Skye** [ˌaɪl‿əv ˈskaɪ] | 2 **Cuillin** [kuːlɪn] | 3 **footprint** [ˈfʊtprɪnt] Fußabdruck | 4 **Portree** [ˈpɔtri] | 5 **Orkney** [ˈɔkni] | 6 **Skara Brae** [ˌskærə ˈbreɪ]

Either:

Read the sentences. Are they true for Orkney or Skye or both?	**Skye**	**Orkney**
1. This is a great place to enjoy nature.		
2. You can visit historical places.		
3. Here you can learn more about a Scottish national language.		
4. Find out how people lived in the Stone Age.		
5. Come here for short nights.		
6. You don't need a boat to come here.		

Or:

Read the text and compare what is mentioned about Skye and Orkney under the headings below.

	Skye	**Orkney**
Geography / Nature		
History		
Culture		

Klett
Green Line 3
Vorschläge zur Leistungsmessung
ISBN: 978-3-12-834234-4

4 Reading: Was that Robert the Bruce?

We've been living in England since I was three, but we still feel Scottish. I was called after[1] a Scottish hero, and when we're staying at Grandma's farm, I dream I'm Robert the Bruce. That's why I like to play in the caves. My grandma says they aren't safe, but my sister and I go anyway. In the evenings Grandma tells us stories of old Scotland and Grandad. We never met him because he died years ago, but Grandma talks about him as if he's still here. Mum says she's lived alone too long and wants her to come and live with us.
On the day that that suggestion was made, Grandma was not happy at all. Flo and I hid in our cave. I was Robert the Bruce and my sister was the spider. She was climbing to the roof of the cave, but suddenly a stone moved and she fell to the floor. More stones fell and some hit me. It was so dark and everything hurt. Then suddenly I saw a man. I knew him. Was it Robert the Bruce? Then somehow[2] we were outside the cave and walking towards the farm. The man was carrying my sister. He gave me water from an old bottle.
A few hours later I woke up in the farmhouse[3].
A doctor was with my sister and my dad said, "Robbie, you've saved your sister's life!"
"It wasn't me," I said. "It was that man."
Then Grandma came in and said, "Robbie, where did you get this bottle? It was Grandpa's."

1 **be called after so** nach jmdm. benannt werden | 2 **somehow** irgendwie | 3 **farmhouse** Bauernhaus

Either:

Read the sentences and tick ✓ the correct answer.

	true	false
1. Robert the Bruce tells the story.		
2. The family moved to England three years ago.		
3. Grandma has been living alone since Grandad died.		
4. Grandma would love to live with her family in England.		
5. Robbie and Flo went to the cave to play Robert the Bruce.		
6. Robert saw a man in the cave before the stones fell.		
7. The unknown man gave Robbie his grandad's old bottle.		

Or:

Read the text and complete the sentences in one to five words.

1. The family moved to England ______________________.
2. Grandma lives ______________________.
3. Grandma doesn't want them to play in the caves because ______________________.
4. Grandma was upset because Mum wanted her ______________________.
5. The accident in the cave happened because Flo tried ______________________.
6. Everybody believes Robbie ______________________.

Green Line 3
Vorschläge zur Leistungsmessung
ISBN: 978-3-12-834234-4

5 Writing: St Andrews

You find this information and these pictures about St Andrews on a new update of Holly's blog. Use them to write a persuasive text about St Andrews.

- 17,000 people live here
- first written about in 7th century
- on coast
- 40 minutes from hills
- 14 miles from Dundee
- lively, historically important
- shops, cafés, golf

6 Writing: An accident!

a) *Look at the picture and write a scene for the story.*

b) *What do you think happens next? Continue the story.*

ISBN: 978-3-12-834234-4

7 Mediation: A visit to Innsbruck

a) *You want to go on holiday with your English friends. You've found this information on the internet, but they need your help to understand it. Answer their questions.*

Innsbruck, die Hauptstadt Tirols, ist der perfekte Ort, um Urlaub zu machen. Diese wunderschöne kleine Großstadt bietet alles für einen Stadtbesuch: Schlendere durch die Altstadt, besichtige das historische Goldene Dachl oder genieße einfach die lebendige Atmosphäre. Einen tollen Blick auf die Stadt bekommt man von der Bergiselschanze, einer 50 Meter hohen Skisprungschanze. Schon seit der Steinzeit haben Menschen im Stadtgebiet von Innsbruck gewohnt und seit ihrer Gründung[1] im Jahre 1180 ist die Stadt zu ihrer heutigen Schönheit herangewachsen.
Um Innsbruck herum ist Natur pur. Hier kann man von den Gebirgen nördlich und südlich der Stadt spektakuläre Aussichten genießen. Für Unternehmungslustige gibt es vielerlei Möglichkeiten, die Tage voll auszunutzen: In unmittelbarer Nähe kann man Klettern gehen. Auch zum Reiten – ob Anfänger oder Weltmeister – oder Fahrradfahren, Mountainbiking oder Trekking liegt Innsbruck in einer idealen Lage.

1 **Gründung** foundation; **gründen** found

Ellis: What is the picture? Is that a ski jump?

You: Yes, ______________________________

Yvonne: What's that about the *Steinzeit*? Was the city built in the Stone Age?

You: ______________________________

Ellis: What can you do in Innsbruck?

You: ______________________________

Yvonne: But I don't want to stay in the city all the time. Can you do anything else?

You: ______________________________

____

Chris: That sounds good. Are the mountains near the city?

You: ______________________________

Yvonne: It says something about riding too. Can you go horse riding near here? Even beginners?

You: ______________________________

▲ **b)** *Your English friends are thinking of visiting Innsbruck. They would like to go sightseeing and do some sport activities too. Write about what they could do there.*

Klett
Green Line 3
Vorschläge zur Leistungsmessung
ISBN: 978-3-12-834234-4

8 Vocabulary: Scotland's choice → (after Station 1)

Look at the picture and think about what is happening. Complete the text with the right words. You can see some words in the picture.

I'm English but I was in Scotland for the r______________ in 2014. It was a fascinating experience for me. I wished was Scottish too. The Scottish people had to choose i______________ or to stay part of the United Kingdom. There was a great atmosphere in the streets – it was like a party. Many people wore k______________ or other traditional clothes. Some people wore t______________ as bracelets around their arms. People waited in a q______________ to vote in a school and a young woman played the b______________ for them. On the floor next to her was a b______________ with a t______________ pattern on it. There were Scottish f______________ everywhere in the streets. It was like a big street party. You could still see posters in shops and on windows from different political p______________. Some said "Vote Yes" and others "Vote No" – no to independence. There was a b______________ which was playing music further up the road. I could just hear the music and I think it was the national a______________ "God Save the Queen". Scotland would need a new n______________ anthem if the people who voted "yes" won.

ISBN: 978-3-12-834234-4

9 Vocabulary: A puzzle → (after Station 2)

a) *Do the crossword.*

Across

1. … is an industry that is important in Glasgow.
6. People usually eat a … with their meat or vegetables.
8. James Watt built the first … engine.
10. A … is somebody who doesn't eat meat (or fish).
11. A … is a person who is from Scotland.
13. Potatoes and carrots are kinds of …
14. Chicken and ham are types of …
15. Scots often eat haggis with … potatoes.
16. You wear a … when it rains.

Down

2. If something isn't allowed, you … it.
3. Penicillin was a very important … which was made by Alexander Fleming.
4. If you are good at Science or Maths, you could think about becoming a …
5. If you … something, you have the idea and design it yourself.
7. You can use a … to lift something which is heavy or to build a house, for example.
9. *Cats* is a … – it's like a play with music.
12. Many roads are so … in Scotland that only one car can drive down them at one time.

b) *Write down your own definitions for these words:*

subject | fill | set off | penicillin | midnight | a close | hundreds (of)

Green Line 3
Vorschläge zur Leistungsmessung
ISBN: 978-3-12-834234-4

10 Language: Who's been writing to you? → (after Station 1)

*Olivia talks to Holly on her mobile. Complete the sentences with **since** or **for** or the correct form of the present perfect progressive.*

Olivia: Hi Holly. ______________________ (you; have) a good time in Scotland?

Holly: Yes, thanks, it's been great. At least we ______________________ (enjoy) ourselves ___________ we arrived. The journey up was terrible.

Olivia: And what about Amber? ______________________ (she; make) friends with Ethan?

Holly: Oh yes, she's in love! She ______________________ (talk) to him or about him ___________ days now.

Olivia: How silly she is! She ______________________ (think) of him ___________ you invited her to go with you.

Holly: Yes, she's silly, but at least she ______________________ (not get) in our way so much.

11 Language: What do you know about Holly? → (after Station 1)

Look at the table and write sentences about Holly in the present perfect progressive.

Who?	What?	Since when / For how long?
1. Holly	go to Thomas Tallis School	she was eleven
2. Holly and Olivia	sit next to each other in classes	their first day at TTS
3. Holly	not wear pink	a few months
4. Holly and Amber	live alone with their mum	dad moved out
5. Holly	not eat meat	she was ten
6. Holly and Amber	stay in Scotland	about a week

1. ______________________________

2. ______________________________

3. ______________________________

4. ______________________________

5. ______________________________

6. ______________________________

Klett
Green Line 3
Vorschläge zur Leistungsmessung
ISBN: 978-3-12-834234-4

12 Language: Rescued from Ben Lomond! → (after Station 2)

Improve this newspaper article about what happened when Gwen and her friends were staying at Loch Lomond! Write the underlined sentences in the passive form. Decide if you need the by-agent.

Last Sunday the Lomond Mountain Rescue Team rescued two young tourists when they were caught in a storm during a walk on Ben Lomond. When the teens started, there wasn't a cloud in the sky, but this changed quickly after they had walked for about an hour. On this mountain the weather can change very quickly. Climbers with experience know this, but tourists often don't know or even ignore this fact.
The two teens had started their walk in the warm morning sun in simple trainers and summer clothes. By 1 p.m. friends who knew their plans saw that there was bad weather up the mountain. When their friends didn't return on time, they called for help. The mountain rescue team started a search for the missing teens right away. They found the two teens at half past three. The young man had fallen and broken his foot. They were both cold and scared. The rescue people took them to hospital and they are both doing well now. People have told them to be more careful next time!

____

____

____

____

____

____

13 Language: Nessie! → (after Station 2)

Complete the gaps in the text with the correct form of the passive.

Stories ________________ (tell) of a monster in Loch Ness as early as the sixth century, but it took a long time until the first photos ________________ (take). Since then Nessie – as she ________________ (know) throughout the world – ________________ (see) many times and many more photos ________________ (take).

But is there really a monster in the loch? The loch is one of the biggest in Scotland. It is over 22 miles long and very deep. There could be an unknown animal in there, but the loch ________________ (search) by scientists many times, and nothing ________________ (find). Every year unknown animals ________________ (find) and described and they ________________ (give) Latin names. You never know: The next one may be called *Nessisauruspopularis*!

Green Line 3
Vorschläge zur Leistungsmessung
ISBN: 978-3-12-834234-4

14 Viewing: The Scottish referendum

a) *Watch and listen to the video and tick ✓ the correct answer.*	true	false
1. The referendum started at 8 o'clock in the morning.		
2. The reporter said that Scotland had a long but hard history.		
3. Before the referendum there was a one-year campaign.		
4. The question was, "Should Scotland be an independent country? Yes or no?"		
5. They flew up the east part of the country.		
6. They flew over mountains.		
7. They flew over spectacular countryside.		

▲ **b)** *Watch again and correct the wrong sentences.*

c) *Look at the pictures and read the sentences. Tick ✓ the things that you hear in the video. More than one answer can be correct.*

1

a) ☐ He voted yes.
b) ☐ He voted no.
c) ☐ He didn't vote.
d) ☐ It's a great chance for the country.
e) ☐ Independence would mean a good future for the kids.

2

a) ☐ She voted yes.
b) ☐ She voted no.
c) ☐ She didn't vote.
d) ☐ She thinks independence will be bad for Scotland.
e) ☐ She thinks they will get independence.

3

a) ☐ He voted yes.
b) ☐ He voted no.
c) ☐ He didn't vote.
d) ☐ It's a great chance for the country.
e) ☐ He's surprised the reporter asks the reason for his decision.

4

a) ☐ They both voted yes.
b) ☐ They both voted no.
c) ☐ One man voted yes and one no.
d) ☐ They are good friends.
e) ☐ They aren't good friends now.

5

a) ☐ She voted yes.
b) ☐ She voted no.
c) ☐ She didn't vote.
d) ☐ She thinks everyone should vote.
e) ☐ She thinks everything will be fine with both results.

Klett
Green Line 3
Vorschläge zur Leistungsmessung
ISBN: 978-3-12-834234-4

Text smart 2: Factual texts

by Nicky Cox Friday, 21st August 2015

HUNTERS[1] are paying thousands of pounds to kill animals in the wild.

This came to the world's attention after a US dentist[2] killed a lion in Zimbabwe, Africa.
Walter Palmer is believed to have paid about £32,000 to kill Cecil the lion. But Cecil was popular with tourists and famous in Africa for being relaxed around people, so the killing caused worldwide horror. Palmer had to go into hiding.
Since the death[3] of Cecil, lots of information has come out about the killing of wild animals for sport, and how much people pay to go on hunts[4]. Cecil's killer, Palmer, is said to be part of a group of American bow-and-arrow[5] hunters who have killed all 29 species of the US's big game animals[6], from polar bears[7] to mountain goats[8].
Before Cecil was killed, a lot of people didn't know what was going on and there has been a huge public outcry[9]. Hunting lions is not against the law[10] in Zimbabwe, and in many other countries in Africa, but hunters have to have special permits, which mean they can kill certain[11] animals.
Some people argue there is a good side to the hunting. They say the money paid by tourists can be used for conservation[12] and to create jobs.

Source: www.firstnews.co.uk

1 **hunter** Jäger | 2 **dentist** Zahnarzt | 3 **death** Tod | 4 **hunt** Jagd; jagen | 5 **bow-and-arrow** Pfeil und Bogen | 6 **game animals** Wildtiere | 7 **polar bear** Eisbär | 8 **mountain goat** Bergziege | 9 **outcry** Aufschrei | 10 **law** Gesetz | 11 **certain** bestimmte/-r/-s | 12 **conservation** Erhaltung

1 Understanding the text

a) *Students have thought of the following headlines for the report. Which one is best?*

1. ☐ Who is killing the lions?
2. ☐ Wild animals in danger from rich hunters
3. ☐ Cecil, the lion king in the wild
4. ☐ Wild animals earn money

b) *Find phrases in the text which have the same meaning. Also write down the line numbers.*

1. Cecil's death shocked people all over the world. ____________________
2. The dentist didn't want people to find him. ____________________
3. In the past not many people knew about these rich hunters. ____________________
4. People are allowed to kill animals in parts of Africa under certain conditions. ____________________
5. It is said that hunting is not all bad for the country. ____________________

2 Elements of a news report

a) *What is the first sentence in this news report trying to do?*

b) *Find three examples of passive constructions in the text.*

Klett
Green Line 3
Vorschläge zur Leistungsmessung
ISBN: 978-3-12-834234-4

Textquellen: Nicky Cox, First News, August 21, 2015

The Countryside Code is a set of rules and advice for people who want to visit the countryside.

The Countryside Code

1. Protect[1] the natural[2] environment:

- leave no trace of your visit and take your rubbish home
- keep dogs under control[3]

2. Enjoy the outdoors:

- plan your trip and be prepared
- follow advice and local signs

3. Consider the local community and other people enjoying the outdoors:

- Respect[4] the needs[5] of local people and visitors – for example, don't block entrances or other paths with your car.
- When riding a bike or driving a car, slow down or stop for horses, walkers and farm animals and give them a lot of room[6]. By law[7], cyclists must give way to walkers and horse-riders on bridleways[8].

Source: www.gov.uk

1 **protect** schützen | 2 **natural** natürlich | 3 **control** Kontrolle | 4 **respect** respektieren | 5 **need** Bedürfnis | 6 **room** hier: Platz | 7 **law** Gesetz | 8 **bridleway** Reitweg

1 Understanding the text

a) *Find a summary for each of the three parts. You don't need two of the summaries.*

- ☐ Leave your bikes, cars, etc. at home.
- ☐ Have fun but think about what you do.
- ☐ Look after nature.
- ☐ Tell others to take care of the environment.
- ☐ Follow the rules and think about others' interests.

b) *Match the phrases from the text with the correct meaning.*

1. leave no trace of your visit
2. enjoy the outdoors
3. consider the local community
4. don't block entrances
5. cyclists must give way to walkers

a) have fun in the countryside
b) take your rubbish with you
c) think about those who live there
d) on some paths people on foot come first
e) don't get in the way of

2 Compare the two factual texts

In which of the two texts can you find these elements? In the box below, underline the elements in 'Hunters' in red and the elements in 'The Countryside Code' in blue.

steps | tells what happened | focuses on facts | several headings | sentences begin with verb | written in present tense | written almost all in past tense | report | instructions

3 Using language

a) *Look at your results for 'The Countryside Code' in exercise 2. What is the text trying to do?*

b) *Underline verbs in the text which show this.*

c) *Why does the text give an example in Line 8 ("… for example, don't block entrances …")?*

Klett
Green Line 3
Vorschläge zur Leistungsmessung
ISBN: 978-3-12-834234-4

Textquellen: From the British government website, Department for Environment, Food & Rural Affairs, October 23, 2014 © Crown copyright

Unit 3: What was it like?

1 Listening: Who were they?

Either:

You are going to hear some people talking about their lives in Britain many years ago. Put the number of the speaker below the correct picture. There is no speaker for one of the pictures.

Elizabeth I  Speaker: ____	A Roman  Speaker: ____	A Celtic man  Speaker: ____
Queen Victoria  Speaker: ____	Henry VIII  Speaker: ____	A Norman  Speaker: ____

Or:

You are going to hear some people talking about their lives in Britain many years ago. Listen and answer the questions below in 1–6 words.

1. Henry VIII is the first speaker. What does he say about the Navy and the Church of England?

   ____

2. What kind of groups did the Celts live in? ______________________
3. Who ruled them? ______________________________
4. What does the third speaker say about The Tower of London?

   ____

5. Why did Elizabeth I never marry? What reason does she give?

   ____

6. Which Roman invention helps us to plan our time? ____________________

Green Line 3
Vorschläge zur Leistungsmessung
ISBN: 978-3-12-834234-4

2 Listening: A class trip to the Globe

Either:
Mr Swindon is telling his class about a trip to the Globe. Listen and note down the important information for the trip:

1. Day of the Trip to the Globe? ______
2. Where to meet? ______
3. When to meet? ______
4. Morning activity? ______
5. Afternoon activity? ______
6. What to wear? ______

Or:
Mr Swindon is telling his class about a trip to the Globe. Listen and tick ✓ the correct answer(s). More than one answer can be correct.

1. When is the class trip to The Globe?
   a) ☐ on Tuesday
   b) ☐ on Thursday
   c) ☐ on Friday

2. How are they going to get there?
   a) ☐ by train
   b) ☐ by underground
   c) ☐ by train and Tube

3. Who thinks the guided tour of the Globe is good?
   a) ☐ Olivia
   b) ☐ Holly
   c) ☐ Mr Swindon

4. When are they going to watch a play?
   a) ☐ in the morning
   b) ☐ after the tour
   c) ☐ in the afternoon

5. What will the weather be like on the day of the class trip?
   a) ☐ cold but dry
   b) ☐ warm and dry
   c) ☐ cold and wet

6. What did people in Shakespeare's day sometimes do while they were watching a play?
   a) ☐ eat
   b) ☐ drink
   c) ☐ throw food

Klett
Green Line 3
Vorschläge zur Leistungsmessung
ISBN: 978-3-12-834234-4

3 Reading: The Industrial Revolution

So you think what happened in the past isn't important for your life now? Then think about this: Why do most people today live in towns and cities? Let's go back to the Industrial Revolution (about 1750–1850), when new inventions changed people's lives forever. Before then, most people had lived in the countryside. They'd worked in the fields or in their homes and had made things by hand. Then new machines were invented that did many of these jobs for them. So many people had to move to towns and cities where the factories were to look for new work. By 1850 about half the people in Britain lived in towns and cities. Today it is about 80%.
Why must all children go to school today? During the time of the Industrial Revolution, many children had to work in the factories too. Some were as young as five years old. They had to work six days each week, often from 6 o'clock in the morning to 8 o'clock in the evening in dangerous conditions, and they were paid very little. But the people they worked for in the factories became very rich. Finally after protests, enough people agreed that this had to change. Children were no longer allowed to work in factories and everybody between the ages of 5 and 13 had to go to school. Conditions for children have improved since then in many places in the world.

Either:
Read the text and complete the sentences in 1–5 words.

1. The Industrial Revolution began in Britain ______________________________.
2. The invention of new machines changed the way people ______________________.
3. Before the 19th century, most people had lived and worked ____________________.
4. With the invention of the new machines, many people lost _____________________.
5. So they had to move to the towns to look for ___________________________.
6. Today about 80% of the people in Britain ______________________________.
7. The children of poor people often had to work 14 hours every day for ______________.
8. Later, things got better and all children from 5 to 13 _________________________.

Or:
Read the text and match the sentence parts. Write the correct letters next to the numbers below.

1. The Industrial Revolution
2. The invention of new machines
3. Before the 19th century, most people
4. Because of new machines many people
5. So these people
6. Life for these people
7. Children often
8. Later, factory owners

a) had lived in the countryside.
b) had to move to the towns to look for work.
c) had to do dangerous work for little money.
d) began in Britain in 1750.
e) weren't allowed to make children work.
f) lost their jobs.
g) changed the way people lived.
h) was very hard.

1. ____ 2. ____ 3. ____ 4. ____ 5. ____ 6. ____ 7. ____ 8. ____

Klett
Green Line 3
Vorschläge zur Leistungsmessung
ISBN: 978-3-12-834234-4

4 Reading: Claire's e-mail to Amy

> Dear Amy,
> Thanks very much for your e-mail and the great photos! It looks like the party was fantastic! ☺
> You remember the project at the community centre that I told you about? Well, yesterday I met with my 'Celts' and my 'Normans'. I was a bit late because I'd had to make an important phone call (which I'd forgotten about earlier) and by the time I got there, there was complete chaos. Just imagine! My Celts were wearing Norman boots, and my Normans had added large bags to their belts for their smartphones!
> Well, I'd just dealt with that problem when one of my Normans, Tom, suddenly shot an arrow through the air and it hit another boy on his head! Luckily, Henry wasn't badly hurt, and we didn't have to call an ambulance, but as soon as he saw blood on his hand, he started to scream. So I had to call his mother and explain what had happened. She was **not** happy!
> By 7 p.m. we were all tired and wanted to go home, but then we found we couldn't get out of the community centre because the main door was locked. So I had to call our drama teacher and ask him to come back and let us out. When the phone rang, he was having a bath. So we had to wait more than half an hour before he finally arrived. Do you have days when everything seems to go wrong too? Please write soon! I can't wait to hear from you again!
> Love, Claire

Either:
Read Claire's e-mail to her friend Amy and answer the questions in 1–6 words.

1. What had Claire done before she went to the community centre? ______________________
2. What was wrong with the Celts' costumes? ______________________
3. Why had the Normans got bags on their belts? ______________________
4. What happened to Henry? ______________________
5. Why couldn't they leave the building? ______________________
6. Why did they have to wait so long for the drama teacher? ______________________

Or:

a) *Read the text and tick ✓ the correct answer.*	true	false
1. Claire was late for her meeting because she'd forgotten about it.		
2. First there was a problem with both the Celts' and the Normans' costumes.		
3. Then Henry was hit on the head by an arrow.		
4. He screamed because he was badly hurt.		
5. Later they couldn't go home because the door was locked.		
6. They had to wait for the drama teacher for more than an hour.		

▲ **b)** *Listen again and correct the wrong sentences.*

Green Line 3
Vorschläge zur Leistungsmessung
ISBN: 978-3-12-834234-4

5 Writing: A person from history

Here is some information about William Shakespeare. Write a short biography.

Name:	William Shakespeare, 1564–1616
Born:	Stratford-upon-Avon, England
Parents:	father glove-maker; mother from rich farming family
Early life:	few details known
Education:	boys' grammar school
Interests:	reading, writing
Family:	marries Anne Hathaway at age 18, three children
Career:	
1590s:	moves to London to become an actor becomes famous as a writer plays very popular, watched by Elizabeth I and King James
1616:	dies at age 52

6 Writing: An interview

a) *For your history project, you have to write an interview with William Shakespeare or Queen Elizabeth I. Write down your questions and his or her answers.*

▲ **b)** *If you were able to travel back in time, which age in history would you travel to? Who would you most like to meet and why? Which questions would you ask this person? You can choose a historical figure like Henry VIII, Elizabeth I, Sir Francis Drake etc. or you can choose a man or a woman who lived in Celtic (Roman/Norman …) times.*

Green Line 3
Vorschläge zur Leistungsmessung
ISBN: 978-3-12-834234-4

7 Mediation: The Tower of London

You are staying with an English family in London. Your host mother Anne has asked you if you would like to visit The Tower of London. You are not sure, so you look for information on the internet. This is what you have found.

Wir4Winter_berlin
Ganz klar ein Highlight unserer Reise nach London. Wir haben viel über die Geschichte von England gelernt. Die Beefeater Tour war sehr lustig und leicht zu verstehen (selbst für Leute, die der englischen Sprache nicht mächtig sind[1]). Wir hatten einen tollen Tag. Aber er war recht teuer. Das nächste Mal werden wir Tickets online kaufen. Und wir werden auch früh da sein, bevor es zu voll wird.

X

1 **einer Sprache nicht mächtig sein** not speak the language very well

Either:
Answer Anne's questions.

Anne: What did the people who wrote this review think about their visit to the Tower?

You: ______________________________

Anne: I can see the words 'Beefeater Tour'. What did they say about it?

You: ______________________________

Anne: Was there anything they didn't like about the tour?

You: ______________________________

Anne: Do you think from what you've read that they'd take part in the tour again?

You: ______________________________

Or:
Tell Anne what these people from Berlin say about their visit to the Tower.

They say it was ______________________________

____

____

____

____

Green Line 3
Vorschläge zur Leistungsmessung
ISBN: 978-3-12-834234-4

8 Vocabulary: Find the words → (after Introduction)

Look at the pictures and write the words.

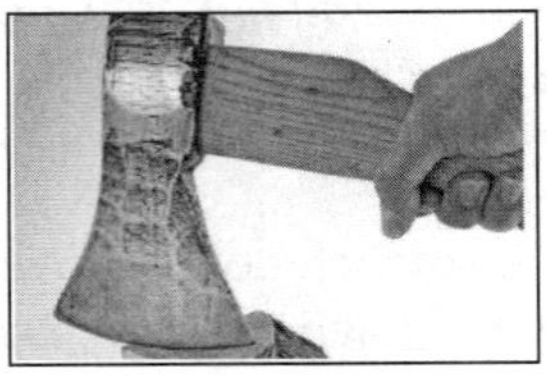

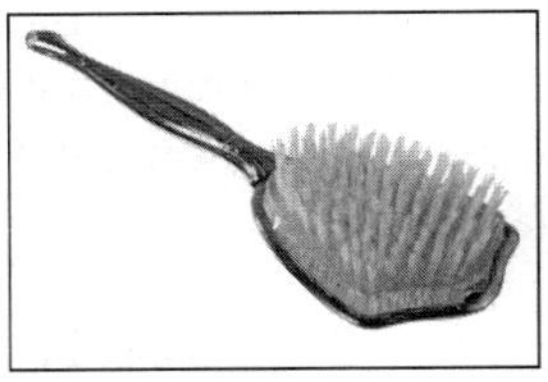

9 Vocabulary: Find the missing word → (after Introduction)

In each line look at the first three words and write down the fourth word.

1. father → mother; son → ________________
2. cinema → film; theatre → ________________
3. near → far; more → ________________
4. England → English; Spain → ________________
5. country → king; empire → ________________

10 Vocabulary: Words with the same meaning → (after Introduction)

Find synonyms (words that have the same meaning).

1. king or queen = ________________
2. to found = ________________
3. loud = ________________
4. to become husband and wife = ________________
5. in those days = ________________
6. to plant (food) = ________________

Green Line 3
Vorschläge zur Leistungsmessung
ISBN: 978-3-12-834234-4

11 Vocabulary: Definitions → (after Station 1)

a) *Fill in the word that belongs to each definition.*

1. a fight between two armies: ________________
2. Someone who belongs to someone else and has to work for them: ________________
3. to become an adult: ________________
4. a piece of jewellery that you wear on your wrist: ________________
5. something that a monarch wears on his/her head: ________________
6. another word for ‘learning : ________________
7. something you can ask if you want a description of a time from the past: ________________

▲ **b)** *Write your own definitions for these words:*

favourite | stage | writer | to experience | to change one's mind

12 Vocabulary: A Beefeater tour → (after Station 2)

Read this part of a Beefeater's tour of the Tower of London. Complete the text with words from the box. There are more words than you need.

period | reign | is made of | is built by | murder | What luck | was built | brought over | blood | forward | dates back to | built | What was it like | emperor

"Behind me, you can see The White Tower. This is the oldest part of the Tower of London and it ________________ the 11th century. It ________________ during the ________________ of William I. As you can see, it ________________ white stone which William ________________ from Normandy in France. The Normans ________________ the Tower as a castle. Later, other English kings added more towers and it became famous as a prison. Over the years, these walls have seen a lot of ______________: Two of Henry VIII's wives lost their heads here, and it was also here that the famous ________________ of Edward IV's two sons took place in 1483. But don't worry! Nothing like that happens here today. ________________ that we live in the 21st century! OK, everybody. Let's move ________________ now."

Green Line 3
Vorschläge zur Leistungsmessung
ISBN: 978-3-12-834234-4

13 Language: Elizabeth I → (after Station 1)

Complete the text with the verbs in brackets. Use the simple past or the past perfect.

When Elizabeth ____________ (become) queen in 1558, after her half-sister Mary ____________ (die), many people ____________ (celebrate) in the streets. They ____________ (be) very happy because Mary, who ____________ (rule) England from 1553 to 1558, ____________ (not be) popular. During Elizabeth's reign, England ____________ (enjoy) a 'golden age' for music, art and drama. It ____________ (be) also a time of great adventure. Sailors like Drake and Raleigh ____________ (sail) to places that English people ____________ (not be) before, and they ____________ (bring) back many treasures which they ____________ (steal) from the Spanish. When Elizabeth ____________ (die) in 1603, England ____________ (become) one of the most powerful and richest countries in the world.

14 Language: The Man in Grey → (after Station 1)

Complete the text with the verbs in brackets. Use the simple past or the past perfect.

Last week Olivia and I ____________ (have) a really weird experience, and all because of Claire. What _______ Claire _______ (do)? She _________ (give) Olivia two theatre tickets and Olivia ____________ (invite) me. I ____________ (be) very excited because I ______________ (never be) to the theatre before. When we ____________ (get) there, we ___________ (go) to our seats[1] in row[2] 4 and ___________ (sit down). At the end of the row we ____________ (notice) a man in a big grey coat[3] and a funny hat who ____________ (look) really strange. Just then we ____________ (have to) stand up because two women ____________ (want) to get by. And when we ____________ (look) again, the man ____________ (go). After the show, we ____________ (tell) Claire what ____________ (happen). "What! You ____________ (see) the Man in Grey!" she ____________ (say) excitedly. "Yes, is he an actor?" Olivia ____________ (ask). "Oh no," Claire ____________ (laugh). "He isn't an actor. He's London's most famous theatre ghost."

1 **seats** Sitzplätze | 2 **row** Reihe | 3 **coat** Mantel

Klett
Green Line 3
Vorschläge zur Leistungsmessung
ISBN: 978-3-12-834234-4

15 Language: If they hadn't … → (after Station 2)

*What would the result have been if some things **hadn't** happened before? Make new sentences with if-clauses type 3.*

1. Olivia and Holly were interested in Elizabeth I, so they joined the Tudor group.

____

2. When Holly was late for the photo shoot, Olivia began to get nervous.

____

3. Olivia had two ladies-in-waiting so that she would look important.

____

4. Holly was late because she had fallen off her skates on the way.

____

5. She had broken her arm and had to wear a plaster cast for the photo.

____

16 Language: Jay is grounded again … → (after Station 2)

Yesterday Mrs Elliot met Mrs Azad and told her about the English test. Now Jay is angry with Luke. Complete their conversation. Use if-clauses type 3.

Jay: My mother ____________________ (never find out) about the English test if your mother ________________ (not tell) her about it yesterday. And if she ____________ ________ (not find out), I __________________ (not be) grounded again.

Luke: Well, I'm really sorry, Jay. But I don't understand why you're angry with *me*.

Jay: I wanted to go to the school disco with Amy on Saturday, and I'm sure that she _________________ (say) 'Yes' if I ________________ (ask) her. But now I can't! If you _________________ (not tell) your mother about the English test, this _________ ______________ (never happen).

Luke: That's not fair, Jay. If you _____________ (work) a bit harder, you ____________ (get) a better mark. And if you ______________ (get) a better mark, you ________ _________ (not be) grounded and you ________________ (can go) to the disco.

Green Line 3
Vorschläge zur Leistungsmessung
ISBN: 978-3-12-834234-4

17 Viewing: Shakespeare and the Globe

a) *Watch the film. Which of these things do you learn about (through words and/or pictures)?*

1. ☐ the location of Globe Theatre
2. ☐ how important and popular it was during Shakespeare's time
3. ☐ why the Globe Theatre has its name
4. ☐ details that show how the theatre is built
5. ☐ the Shakespeare plays that are performed every year
6. ☐ Sometimes it was dangerous to watch a play!

b) *Watch the film again and tick ✓ the correct answer(s). More than one answer can be correct.*

1. Who reigned in England during Shakespeare's time?
   a) ☐ Queen Victoria
   b) ☐ Henry VIII
   c) ☐ Queen Elizabeth

2. Which quote(s) do you hear in the film?
   a) ☐ "To be or not to be, that is the question."
   b) ☐ "All the world's a stage …"
   c) ☐ "Fair is foul and foul is fair."

3. Which of these statements about the Globe is/are true?
   a) ☐ It has high outside walls.
   b) ☐ There's no roof over the central part.
   c) ☐ The stage is open on only one side.

4. Where was the audience during a play?
   a) ☐ Some sat where they could look down on the stage.
   b) ☐ Some stood behind the stage.
   c) ☐ Some stood next to the stage.

5. Why are Shakespeare's plays interesting for us today?
   a) ☐ They are better than modern plays.
   b) ☐ They bring people to the theatre.
   c) ☐ They show how people were back then.

6. How many people could watch a play at one time?
   a) ☐ a third of all Londoners
   b) ☐ 2,000 people
   c) ☐ 20,000 people

7. What caused problems for some people?
   a) ☐ robbers
   b) ☐ bad weather
   c) ☐ things being thrown from the stage

8. What is said about Shakespeare and the actors?
   a) ☐ He didn't think about the actors when he wrote.
   b) ☐ They didn't really know each other.
   c) ☐ He made parts specially for them.

▲ **c)** *Why do you think the speaker uses the present tense to talk about a scene from the past?*

Green Line 3
Vorschläge zur Leistungsmessung
ISBN: 978-3-12-834234-4

B
A

B
A

A *Look at both pictures closely. For each one:*
- *Describe the situation and say what the people are doing.*
- *Say what the people might be thinking or feeling. Give reasons.*

A1

A2

 ISBN 978-3-12-834234-4

SPEAKING 1

B *Look at both pictures closely. For each one:*
- *Describe the situation and say what the people are doing.*
- *Say what the people might be thinking or feeling. Give reasons.*

B1

B2

Klett
© Ernst Klett Verlag GmbH, Stuttgart 2016.
Alle Rechte vorbehalten. ISBN 978-3-12-834234-4

1 SPEAKING

Partner A: *With your partner, choose one of the situations in the four pictures and do a role play:*

A1
You are the coach and your partner is the player who is talking to him. The game is going badly. Give the team advice: How can they still win this game?

A2
You are one of the dance teachers and your partner is one of the dancers who is having problems. Give your partner advice: What should he/she do?

B1
You are the teacher and your partner is one of the actors. The show didn't go well. Give your partner advice: What should he/she do for tomorrow's show? Try to find a compromise.

B2
You are the girl at the desk and your partner is one of her friends. Explain to your partner why you can't go to the party. Try to find a compromise with your friends.

Klett
© Ernst Klett Verlag GmbH, Stuttgart 2016.
Alle Rechte vorbehalten. ISBN 978-3-12-834234-4

SPEAKING 1

Partner B: *With your partner, choose one of the situations in the four pictures and do a role play:*

A1
You are the player who is talking to the coach and your partner is the coach. Explain to your partner why the game is going badly.

A2
You are one of the dancers who is having problems and your partner is one of the dance teachers. Explain to your partner what problems you are having.

B1
You are one of the actors and your partner is the teacher. The show didn't go well. Explain to your partner why you don't want to perform again tomorrow. Try to find a compromise.

B2
You are one of the girl's friends and your partner is the girl at the desk. Explain to your partner why she should come to the party. Try to find a compromise.

Klett
© Ernst Klett Verlag GmbH, Stuttgart 2016.
Alle Rechte vorbehalten. ISBN 978-3-12-834234-4

A *Look at both pictures closely. Then:*
- *Describe the situation in each picture.*
- *Name things in the pictures that are "typically Scottish".*
- *Say what is similar/different about how the pictures show the Scottish.*

 ISBN 978-3-12-834234-4

SPEAKING 2

B *Look at both pictures closely. Then:*
- *Describe the situation in each picture.*
- *Name things in the pictures that are "typically German".*
- *Say what is similar/different about how the pictures show the Germans.*

 ISBN 978-3-12-834234-4

2 SPEAKING

Partner A/B (Set 1): *You and your partner are planning a two-week trip to Scotland. You've seen these four pictures in a travel brochure:*

Loch Ness

Duart Castle

Aberdeen Jazz Festival

Shipbuilding in Glasgow

- *Discuss which places you'd like to visit and what you would like to do there. If you have other ideas, you can talk about those too!*
- *Discuss how long you want to stay in each place.*
- *Discuss what information you need to find out about these places to prepare for your trip.*

 ISBN 978-3-12-834234-4

SPEAKING 2

Partner A/B (Set 2): *You and your partner are planning a two-week trip to Scotland. You've seen these four pictures in a travel brochure:*

Ben Nevis

Edinburgh

Aberdeen Highland Games

Loch Lomond

- *Discuss which places you'd like to visit and what you would like to do there. If you have other ideas, you can talk about those too!*
- *Discuss how long you want to stay in each place.*
- *Discuss what information you need to find out about these places to prepare for your trip.*

 ISBN 978-3-12-834234-4

B

A

A/B

A/B

B

A

A/B

A/B

A *You took a trip back in time with your time machine. When you were there you tried to hide and watch the people, but someone saw you! You got home just in time! Talk about what you saw on your trip and what adventures you had.*

B *You took a trip back in time with your time machine. When you were there you tried to hide and watch the people, but someone saw you! You got home just in time! Talk about what you saw on your trip and what adventures you had.*

Klett
© Ernst Klett Verlag GmbH, Stuttgart 2016.
Alle Rechte vorbehalten. ISBN 978-3-12-834234-4

Partner A/B (Set 1): *Oh no! The time machine has brought Partner A from the past into the present with Partner B. Together, find out about each other and about what has happened, and discuss how to get out of this difficult situation.*

Klett
© Ernst Klett Verlag GmbH, Stuttgart 2016.
Alle Rechte vorbehalten. ISBN 978-3-12-834234-4

Partner A/B (Set 2): *Oh no! The time machine has brought Partner A from the past into the present with Partner B. Together, find out about each other and about what has happened, and discuss how to get out of this difficult situation.*

Klett
© Ernst Klett Verlag GmbH, Stuttgart 2016.
Alle Rechte vorbehalten. ISBN 978-3-12-834234-4

A Your family is talking about your next summer holiday. Your parents aren't very excited about the idea of a beach holiday. What are they worried about? Describe the situations in the picture.

 ISBN 978-3-12-834234-4

4 SPEAKING

B Your family is talking about your next summer holiday. Your parents aren't very excited about the idea of a boat trip. What are they worried about? Describe the situations in the picture.

 ISBN 978-3-12-834234-4

4 SPEAKING

Partner A: Your parents want you and your brother/sister to decide where to go on your next summer holiday. You love nature and outdoor sports and so you'd like to go camping in the mountains. You don't like airplane trips and travelling to big cities, but your sister/brother loves big cities and wants to visit one.
Argue for your idea and against your partner's. Both of you need to agree on a place before you can talk to your parents.

 ISBN 978-3-12-834234-4

4 SPEAKING

Partner B: Your parents want you and your brother/sister to decide where to go on your next summer holiday. You want to see the world and so you'd like go to a big city! You think nature trips are boring, but your brother/sister wants to go camping in the mountains.
Argue for your idea and against your partner's. Both of you need to agree on a place before you can talk to your parents.

 ISBN 978-3-12-834234-4

B
A

B
A

Text smart 3: Fictional texts

A monster calls

by Patrick Ness

The monster came just after midnight. As they do.

Conor was awake[1] when it came.

He'd had a nightmare[2]. Well, not *a* nightmare. *The* nightmare. The one he'd been having a lot recently The one with the darkness and the wind and the screaming. The one with the hands slipping from[3] him, no matter how hard he tried to hold on. The one that always ended with –

"Go away," Conor whispered into the darkness of his bedroom, trying to push the nightmare back, not let it follow him into the world of waking[4]. "Go away now."

He looked over at the clock his mum had put on the table next to his bed. 12:07. Seven minutes past midnight. Which was late for a school night, late for a Sunday, anyway.

He'd told nobody about the nightmare. Not his mum, of course, but nobody else either[5], not his dad in their twice monthly (or so) phone call, *definitely* not his grandma, and nobody at school. Absolutely not. What happened in the nightmare was something nobody else ever needed to know.

Conor blinked[6] sleepily at his room, then he frowned[7]. There was something he was missing. He sat up in his bed, waking a bit more. The nightmare was slipping from him, but there was something he couldn't put his finger on[8], something different, something –

He listened very hard against the silence, but all he could hear was the quiet house around him, a rustle[9] of bedding[10] from his mum's room next door.

Nothing.

And then something. Something he realised was the thing that had woken him.

Someone was calling his name.

Conor.

He felt a sudden panic, his stomach twisting[11]. Had it followed him? Had it somehow stepped out of the nightmare and – ?

"Don't be stupid," he told himself. "You're too old for monsters."

And he was. He'd had his thirteenth birthday just last month. Monsters were for babies. Monsters were for bed-wetters[12]. Monsters were for –

Conor.

There it was again. Conor swallowed[13]. His window was still open. Maybe the curtains[14] in the light wind could have sounded like –

Conor.

OK, it wasn't the wind. It was definitely a voice, but not one he knew. It wasn't his mother's, that was for sure[15]. It wasn't a woman's voice at all, and he asked himself for a crazy moment if his dad somehow made a surprise trip from America and arrived too late to phone and –

Conor.

No. Not his dad. This voice had a quality to it, a *monstrous* quality, wild and untamed[16].

Then he heard a heavy creak[17] of wood outside, as if something really huge was stepping across a wooden floor.

He didn't want to go and look. But at the same time, a part of him wanted to look more than anything.

1 **awake** wach | 2 **nightmare** Albtraum | 3 **slip from** entgleiten | 4 **wake** aufwachen | 5 **not either** auch nicht | 6 **blink** blinzeln | 7 **frown** die Stirn runzeln | 8 **can't put your finger on sth** etw. nicht genau sagen können | 9 **rustle** Rascheln | 10 **bedding** Bettwäsche | 11 **twist** verdrehen | 12 **bed-wetter** Bettnässer | 13 **swallow** schlucken | 14 **curtain** Vorhang | 15 **for sure** mit Sicherheit | 16 **untamed** ungezähmt | 17 **creak** Knarren

Green Line 3
Vorschläge zur Leistungsmessung
ISBN: 978-3-12-834234-4

Textquellen: From *A Monster Calls* by Patrick Ness, Walker Books, London, May 5, 2011

1 Understanding the text

a) *Finish the sentences with these words from the text. You don't need all of the words.*

darkness (l. 6) | hold on (l. 9) | missing (l. 28) | silence (l. 32) | realised (l. 37) | stomach (l. 41) | sounded (l. 53) | voice (l. 56) | stepping (l. 67)

1. He had a pain in his _____________ because he was so nervous.
2. There were no sounds at all; only _____________.
3. Without moonlight he could see nothing in the _____________.
4. He could hear something _____________ across the room and making funny noises.
5. He couldn't explain the situation because part of what he needed to know was _____________.

b) *Put the events of the night in the correct order (1–7).*

Conor sits up and finds out that something is different. But what? _____
Something big is moving outside. _____
Conor hears his name for the first time. _____
Conor wakes up. _____
Conor realises that he is hearing a voice he doesn't know. _____
Conor has a nightmare. _____
Conor tells himself there are no monsters. _____

c) *What do you find out about Conor?*

2 Elements of fictional texts

1. The narrative perspective

a) *What can you say about the narrator? (Type? Perspective?)*

b) *If the text was written from another perspective, what differences could there be? Name two things. (Think about the place, feelings, characters.)*

2. The senses

a) *Which of the five senses (see, hear, smell, touch, taste) is most important in this text?*

b) *Are any other senses mentioned in the text? Give examples with line numbers from the text.*

3. Suspense

a) *How does the writer create suspense? Tick ✓ the features which go with this text.*

☐ science fiction
☐ things we don't understand yet
☐ something surprising and scary
☐ fast action
☐ reader shares a character's fear
☐ fighting and violence
☐ descriptions with lots of detail
☐ ending at a dramatic moment
☐ quick changes of scene
☐ important word repeated

▲ **b)** *What do you think will happen next? Why? Write at least four sentences.*

Klett
Green Line 3
Vorschläge zur Leistungsmessung
ISBN: 978-3-12-834234-4

Unit 4 On the move

1 Listening: At the airport

Either:

Listen to the dialogues and match them to the pictures. There's one extra picture.

Dialogue ________________

Dialogue ________________

Dialogue ________________

Dialogue ________________

Dialogue ________________

Dialogue ________________

Or:

a) *Listen to the dialogues and tick ✓ the correct answer.*	**true**	**false**
1. Dialogue 1: The passengers may not use mobile phones.		
2. Dialogue 2: The flight attendant wants to see the boy's passport and boarding card.		
3. Dialogue 2: Boarding has already started.		
4. Dialogue 3: Flight 924 has a delay.		
5. Dialogue 3: The passengers are asked to wait at the gate.		
6. Dialogue 4: The girl would like to sit near the window.		
7. Dialogue 4: The plane will leave from gate 42 at quarter past ten.		
8. Dialogue 5: The boy will meet his mother in the arrivals hall in about one hour.		

▲ **b)** *Listen again and correct the wrong sentences.*

ISBN: 978-3-12-834234-4

2 Listening: "True" stories

Either:

a) *Listen to the conversation and write the letters of the correct pictures in the order that you hear them. Two pictures don't show exactly what is told.*

Correct order: ____________________

b) *Explain why the two pictures are wrong.*

____

____

Or:

Read these statements. Then listen to the conversation. Cross out the words that are wrong and correct them in 1–6 words.

1. One plane couldn't land because of the bad weather. ____________________
2. One plane had to land because the pilot was ill. ____________________
3. One pilot asked the passengers to push the plane to the terminal. ____________________
4. Usually airport workers push the plane away from the building. ____________________
5. A plane couldn't leave once because a passenger was still outside. ____________________
6. A passenger was asked to sit on the toilet because he was ill. ____________________

Green Line 3
Vorschläge zur Leistungsmessung
ISBN: 978-3-12-834234-4

3 Reading: Friends for life?

A I was really excited about our exchange to Germany. My exchange partner sounded really nice and we had lots of similar interests, like horses and sport. Munich sounded great too and I love to speak foreign languages.

B When we arrived at Munich airport, Leonie and her parents were there and they were excited to meet me. They spoke in German, but I didn't understand everything, so I said, "Wie bitte?" Then they spoke English. I was disappointed.
The next day the parents only spoke to me in almost perfect English. Leonie's English is also very good, so she spoke only English to me too. I wasn't happy about it but I didn't know what to do.

C A few days later it was getting on my nerves and so I spoke to my teacher about it. She suggested that I talk to Leonie and her parents. She said that they wouldn't be upset if I asked them politely to speak German with me. Sunday evening after dinner I told them how I felt. I was really embarrassed, but they were very good about it. We talked all evening and laughed too. I found out that there were things they found difficult too. They said they would be happier if I were more honest and less polite.

D Two weeks later I went home – sad and happy. Sad to leave, but what a great experience! My German had improved, I had some new friends and I think I'd learnt something for life!

Either:
Read the text and answer the questions in 1–6 words.

1. What hobbies do Gemma and Leonie have? ______
2. Where did Gemma's plane land? ______
3. How did Gemma feel when Leonie's parents spoke English to her? ______
4. What did Gemma's teacher say she should do? ______
5. How did Leonie s family feel after Gemma had told them her problem? ______
6. What did Leonie's family want? How could Gemma change? ______

Or:
Read the text and fill in the table.

When?	How did Gemma feel?	Why?
Before the trip		
At the end of the first day		
On Sunday evening		
Two weeks later		

Green Line 3
Vorschläge zur Leistungsmessung
ISBN: 978-3-12-834234-4

4 Reading: A new life

"Oh, look at all those people on one boat. I couldn't do that. I'd be too scared," I said. "Yes, but you have to think about what they are running away from. There's war in their countries. They have nothing to eat, no future." Dad said they had no choice. He looked sad, but he knew what it was like to have to leave his own country. He had told me his story many times. Dad was born in a country that he wasn't allowed to leave without a visa. Dad was happy enough there, but he wanted to travel and see the world. He was a photographer and he still is. One year he had to go to another country to take photos for two weeks. A whole team was going and this was Dad's chance to get away. After he had worked for a week and earned some money, he left the team at midnight and went straight to the airport. He didn't have a plane ticket or a visa, so he just had to wait in the airport. He lived there for a week. He had little money, but people gave him food. He became friends with the people who worked there and slept on the chairs. Then he got his chance. An English teacher gave my dad his own passport and ticket. So how did he get through passport control with somebody else's passport? Dad told me that at that time the people who worked there often didn't really look at your face. It would be very different now. Dad was never sorry that he came to live in England, but he was always sad that he never saw his parents again. He later found the teacher and thanked him for his new life.

Either:

Read the story about Adita's father's life and put the sentences in the correct order.

1. In the end he was given somebody else's passport and a ticket.
2. He thanked the teacher.
3. He slept on the seats at the airport.
4. He travelled to a different country and took photos there.
5. Adita's dad wanted to travel around the world.
6. He got on a plane to England.
7. In the middle of the night Adita's dad went to the airport.

Correct order: ______________________________

Or:

Find the following information in the text. Write down the line numbers and quote from the text. There is one example.

1. Adita was talking to her dad about refugees at sea. 1–5: "Oh, look … no future."
2. Adita's dad had been a refugee. ______________
3. He earns money by taking photos. ______________
4. He used the chance of a business trip to get away. ______________
5. He made friends with the airport workers. ______________
6. A teacher helped Adita's dad to get to England. ______________
7. Adita's dad lives in England. ______________

Green Line 3
Vorschläge zur Leistungsmessung
ISBN: 978-3-12-834234-4

5 Writing: It's fun to travel

Choose one of the pictures and use the tips to write a short dialogue between the two people.

Tip:
- What is happening?
- How could the people in the picture feel?
- What could they say?
- Remember to be polite.

____

____

____

____

____

6 Writing: A travel report

a) *Look at the two photos and choose one of them. You are one of the people in the photo. Write a report about what has happened.*

Think about these questions:
- What has happened?
- Where have you been and where are you going to?
- How are the people in the photo feeling?

____

____

____

____

____

____

▲ **b)** *Look at the pictures for "True stories" (p. 44) again. Choose one and write a dialogue between two people (at least 6 sentences).*

ISBN: 978-3-12-834234-4

7 Mediation: What did she say?

You are staying with friends of your parents' in England and your sister is on her way back to Germany. She's just sent you an e-mail from the airport.

Hi,
Du wirst es nicht glauben, aber ich bin immer noch hier am Heathrow Flughafen – vier Stunden nachdem ihr mich abgesetzt habt. Alles ist schiefgegangen!
Ich hatte meine Bordkarte schon und bin direkt zur Passkontrolle gegangen. Die waren zwar sehr freundlich, haben aber nicht wirklich geglaubt, dass es mein Pass war – ich habe mich schon ein bisschen verändert in den letzten paar Jahren! Am Ende ließen sie mich doch durch und dann musste ich zur Sicherheitskontrolle. Das war so unangenehm. Jean hatte mir die Flasche hausgemachte Limonade gegeben, aber man darf keine Flüssigkeiten mitnehmen. Deshalb habe ich sie sofort ausgetrunken. Sage Jean, dass es sehr lecker war! Dann war ich allerdings ziemlich spät dran und musste zum Gate rennen.
Ich habe es gerade noch ins Flugzeug geschafft, bevor das Gate geschlossen wurde. Ich war total froh, als ich mich endlich hinsetzen durfte. Dann aber warteten wir und warteten bis der Pilot endlich sagte, dass es ein Problem mit dem Flugzeug gibt.
Deshalb sitze ich jetzt hier in den Abflughalle und warte. Es ist aber nicht so schlimm. Mein Sitznachbar ist sehr nett – er ist Engländer und besucht Deutschland zum ersten Mal. Ich werde seine Reisebegleiterin sein, aber erzähle Jean das nicht. Sie würde sich nur Sorgen machen!
LG, Lea.

Your host walks in after you read the mail. Answer her questions.

Jean: Where is Lea now?

You: ______________________________

____

Jean: Why? What happened?

You: ______________________________

Jean: Oh no. But did everything else go well?

You: ______________________________

____

____

Jean: What is she doing now?

You: ______________________________

Jean: Ohhhh …

You: But she says ______________________________. And she told me to say ______________________________.

Green Line 3
Vorschläge zur Leistungsmessung
ISBN: 978-3-12-834234-4

8 Vocabulary: At the airport → (after Introduction)

What can you see? Write the correct words next to the picture.

1. ____________________
2. ____________________
3. ____________________
4. ____________________
5. ____________________
6. ____________________
7. ____________________
8. ____________________

9 Vocabulary: What's the word? → (after Station 1)

a) *Match the definitions and the words.*

1. athletics ________
2. vending machine ________
3. spill ________
4. Hang on! ________
5. abroad ________
6. garlic ________
7. sleep ________
8. coast ________

a) vegetable with a strong taste and smell
b) Wait a moment!
c) in a foreign country
d) land which is next to the sea
e) sports where you run, jump or throw things
f) You need this so you are not tired.
g) when your drink falls out of your glass
h) You can buy drinks from here. Just put a coin in.

▲ **b)** *Write your own definitions for these words.*

soup: ____________________

hostel: ____________________

mutter: ____________________

Green Line 3
Vorschläge zur Leistungsmessung
ISBN: 978-3-12-834234-4

10 Vocabulary: Word pairs → (after Station 2)

Find the word pairs. Say if the words have the same meaning (=) or opposite meanings (≠.)

get in | security | out of | arrivals | purpose | search for | take-off | truth

1. departures ______________________________
2. lie ______________________________
3. look for ______________________________
4. danger ______________________________
5. get out ______________________________
6. in ______________________________
7. reason ______________________________
8. landing ______________________________

11 Language: A trip by train! → (after Station 1)

You and your partner want to write an article about people in a train station. It's your job to go to the train station and listen, and then report back to your partner what the people said. Look at the speech bubbles and complete the sentences.

1. Young man on phone:
"I'm still waiting for the train!"

2. Young woman to old woman:
"My daughter will help me with my suitcases."

3. Mother to her son:
"You can't have any chips. You've just eaten three sandwiches."

4. Old man to young man:
"I wanted to build trains when I was a child."

5. Girl on phone:
"Yes Mum. I'll call as soon as I arrive in France."

6. Boy to a man he has run into:
"I'm very sorry but I didn't see you."

1. The young man said that ______________________________.
2. A young woman said that her daughter ______________________________.
3. A woman told her son that he ______________________________.

   She said that he ______________________________.
4. An old man said that he ______________________________.
5. A girl told her mum that ______________________________ as soon as she arrived in France.
6. A boy apologised to a man and said ______________________________.

Green Line 3
Vorschläge zur Leistungsmessung
ISBN: 978-3-12-834234-4

12 Language: Lucy's class goes to France → (after Station 1)

Lucy's class went to France on a class trip. The students talked about all sorts of different things. After the trip Lucy tells her mother about it. What did the students say? Complete the sentences.

"I want to stay here this evening," said Steve.
"Oh, we can stay in tomorrow after training. I'd like to explore today," said Patrick.
"I've forgotten to bring batteries for my camera," said Emily.
"You can buy them tomorrow," I said.
"My cat was very ill yesterday so I didn't want to come here," said Luke.
"Your mum told me about it. She said you shouldn't worry. You'll see him next week," I said.

We all had a good journey to France but when we got there everybody talked about their problems.

At the hostel Steve said that he wanted to stay ____________________, but Patrick said that

they could stay in ____________ after training. He wanted to explore ________________. Then

the other problems started. Emily said she'd forgotten to ______________ batteries. I told her that

____________ could buy them ___________________. Then Luke said that his cat had been

very ill ____________ and that he hadn't wanted to go _________________. His mum had told

me about it and so I said he shouldn't worry and that he would see his cat _______________.

13 Language: At the end of the trip → (after Station 2)

The athletics team is going home tomorrow. The coach and the team have lots of questions. Kate is texting and doesn't hear any of the questions. You report the questions for her later.

Coach: Have you all had a good time?

You: ____

Coach: What did you like best?

You: ____

Luke: When will we arrive home?

You: ____

Coach: Are you all happy to return home?

You: ____

Luke: Do we have to pack our things now?

You: ____

Green Line 3
Vorschläge zur Leistungsmessung
ISBN: 978-3-12-834234-4

14 Language: On the ferry → (after Station 2)

Lucy's class are on the ferry. They're going back to England. Report the commands and requests.

1. "Don't run." → The man told them ______________________________.
2. "Listen to the security instructions."

   →The captain told passengers ______________________________.
3. "Please don't throw any rubbish in the sea."

   They were asked ______________________________.
4. "Please help me with my bags." → A girl asked a man ______________________________.
5. "Please go to your cars now." → The captain told passengers ______________________________.

15 Language: The French exchange → (after Station 2)

Sophie is in France on a French exchange. She called her mum on the phone and now her mum reports the conversation to her grandma. Complete the sentences.

Sophie:	Yes, I'm having a great time. We've eaten lots of interesting food.
Mum:	Oh, what have you eaten?
Sophie:	Yesterday we had a really good garlic soup! And do you know that French teenagers drink wine with their meals?
Mum:	Well, you mustn't drink wine, Sophie. You're only 14 and anyway, I'm sure not all French teenagers drink wine.
Sophie:	Oh Mum! Anyway, I'll call you on Friday. I can't call tomorrow. I'm going to a disco with some friends.
Mum:	Well, don't stay out too late, Sophie and …
Sophie:	Oh, Mum. Sorry. I have to go now. Bye. I'll call again.

Grandma: So is Sophie happy in France?

Mum: Yes, she called on Sunday and said she ____________ a great time. She said that she ____________ lots of interesting food. I asked her ____________________ and she answered that they ______________ a good garlic soup ______________. Then she asked ______________ that French teenagers ______________ wine with their meals! Of course, I told her ____________ any wine and I said that I ______________ that not all French teenagers drank wine. Then she said she ______________ on Friday and that she ______________ the next day because she ________________ to a disco with some friends. I told her ______________ too late but then she just said goodbye. That was it!

Klett
Green Line 3
Vorschläge zur Leistungsmessung
ISBN: 978-3-12-834234-4

Text smart 4 Drama

An important decision

(Scene: Outside the sports club after training. Henry and Max come in from the left, carrying their sports bags. Julie and Emily come from the right and meet them.)

Julie: Hi, you guys! You two look very tired! Given your all for the team again?

Henry: Of course! That was our last training before the big match on Saturday.

Emily: Have you chosen the team yet, Henry?

Henry: Just about. I'll decide tomorrow.

Julie: *(babyish voice)* Put little Max on the team this time, PLEASE!! He tries SOO hard!

(She pats[1] Max on the head, and he pushes her off angrily.)

Max: Stop it! I'm not a baby! *(turning to Henry)* But Julie's right. – I'm SO keen to play.

Henry: You're getting on my nerves, Max. Just get this straight: I have to choose the very best players. And you're not in the top eleven.

Max: I guess that guy Nathan is on the team.

Emily: Who's Nathan?

Julie: I know! I've seen him. He's a new boy and he's really cute.

Henry: Maybe he is. Anyway, he's a fantastic footballer. Look – here he is now.

(Nathan comes in from the left, carrying his sports bag.)

Julie: *(whispering to Emily)* See what I mean?

Henry: Nathan, you're on the team for Saturday, OK?

Nathan: No, sorry. I can't play in the next match.

Henry: *(shocked)* What?!!

Emily: *(worried)* Are you injured[2]?

Nathan: No, no. But I've got an important music exam in two weeks, so I can't do any risky[3] sport till that's over.

Max: You make music?

Nathan: Yes, I play the violin[4].

(Short pause. Then Max bursts out laughing. He pretends to play the violin.)

Emily: What is there to laugh at? What's wrong with playing the violin?

Henry: *(angry)* You mean you'll give up a place on our team just to mess around[5] on a violin?

Max: Don't worry, Henry. You've still got me for the team.

Julie: That's right! Music for Nathan, a place on the team for Max – and everyone's happy!

Henry: Not me! Look here, Nathan. If you train with us, you have to be there for matches. So make up your mind: violin exam or football. I'll give you until tomorrow.

Emily: I don't understand, Henry. Why are you so upset? Nathan will only miss one match –

Max: *(interrupting)* – and I'm ready to play instead.

Henry: Oh, do shut up, Max!

Julie: All this argument about a football match! Come on, Emily – let's go to the café. You too, Nathan.

(Julie takes Nathan by the arm; she and Emily go off to the right. Max is undecided[6]; Henry goes off to the left and calls after Nathan)

Henry: Don't forget, Nathan! Tomorrow is your last chance!

1 **pat** tätscheln | 2 **injured** verletzt | 3 **risky** riskant | 4 **violin** Geige | 5 **mess around** herumspielen | 6 **undecided** unentschlossen

Green Line 3
Vorschläge zur Leistungsmessung
ISBN: 978-3-12-834234-4

1 Understanding the text

a) *Find phrases in the text which have the same meaning as the underlined words. The numbers in brackets give you the lines where you can find the context for the meaning of the phrases.*

1. You've tried as hard as possible, but it isn't enough. ____________________ (5–10)
2. We have almost finished tidying up. Only the cupboard now. ____________________ (11–14)
3. Now please understand what I'm saying. – The answer is no! ____________________ (20–25)
4. You can't have both. Choose the one or the other. ____________________ (59–63)
5. Can't you stop talking for just one minute? ____________________ (67–72)

b) *Complete the sentences with information from the text.*

1. Next Saturday there will be ____.
2. Henry has to choose ____.
3. Max would like to ____.
4. Nathan says he can't play for the team because ____.
5. Henry says Nathan must choose ____.
6. Emily and Julie can't understand ____.

2 Elements of a dramatic text

a) *Look at the characters in this scene. Who is described in each sentence? Fill in the letters a)–e). A sentence can fit more than one character.*

1. teases Max ________
2. has not known the others very long ________
3. takes his/her role very seriously ________
4. tries to see different points of view ________
5. doesn't take other people's hobbies seriously ________
6. must choose between two chances ________

a) Julie
b) Henry
c) Emily
d) Max
e) Nathan

▲ **b)** *How could the situation develop? What do you think? How will Nathan decide? Why? Write at least four sentences.*

Klett
Green Line 3
Vorschläge zur Leistungsmessung
ISBN: 978-3-12-834234-4

1 The French exam

Next week is exam week at TTS. Jay's French teacher is giving him some advice. What does he tell him? Complete the text. Use conditional clauses type 1. Use short forms where possible.

"Jay, if you ____________ (work) hard, you ____________ (do) well next week.

It ____________ (help) if you ____________ (learn) the vocabulary and if you ______________

(look at) the irregular verbs again. Before you start the exam, read the questions carefully and make

notes. If you ______________ (do) that, you _____________ (not give) the wrong answers. And

don't work too quickly this time. If you _____________ (work) too fast,

you ____________ (make) silly mistakes again. Oh, and make sure that I can read your writing.

If I ______________ (not be able to) read what you have written, you ____________ (get) a bad

mark. And just one final piece of advice, Jay: If you ____________ (copy) from your neighbour,

or if he _____________ (copy) from you again, both of you _____________ (be) in real trouble."

2 What will happen to me if you leave, Shahid?

Complete this conversation between Jay and Shahid. Use conditional clauses type 1. Use short forms where possible.

Jay: Are you going to move out when you finish your studies, Shahid?

Shahid: I don't know yet. If I ____________ (get) a job in London, I ____________ (stay) here for a while. But if somebody ____________ (offer) me a good job in another city, then I ____________ (have to) move out.

Jay: Oh no! If that ____________ (happen), Shahid, I ____________ (be) here all on my own and ____________ (go) crazy.

Shahid: No, you won't, Jay. If I ____________ (move away), you ____________ (still – have) all your friends here.

Jay: That's what you think. I ____________ (not have) any friends left if I ____________ (be grounded) every week, will I?

Shahid: Then follow the rules. If you ____________ (follow) the rules, you ________________ (not be grounded). It's as simple as that.

Green Line 3
Vorschläge zur Leistungsmessung
ISBN: 978-3-12-834234-4

3 Stars UK

Stars UK is a TV show for new talents. Here is what happened to one girl when she broke the rules. Complete the text with the correct forms of the verbs. Use the simple past or the present perfect.

Yesterday the makers of Stars UK __________ (throw) Hannah Bird out of the competition when viewers ___________ (go) online and ___________ (find out) the true story about her. The TV show is for new talents, but Hannah ________________ (already work) as a singer. On her website, Hannah describes how she _______________ (already sing) in three different musicals and says that two years ago she even ____________ (sing) the lead in Evita. After the show last night there __________ (be) a lot of angry voices on social media sites. Izzy from Greenwich ____________ (write): "So far I ____________ (be) a fan of Stars UK, but I ________________ (not watch) the show since I found out about Hannah. So upset." Many others agree with her. "Do they think we're idiots?" another __________ (ask). "That's it. I __________ (have) enough!"

4 The life of the fashion designer Victoria Beckham

Complete the text with the verbs in the correct forms. Use the simple past or the present perfect.

Victoria Beckham __________ (be) very lucky in her life so far and she __________ (have) a lot of success. She says it is because she ____________ (always work) hard; she ____________ (never give up) and she _____________ (always believe) in herself. Her career __________ (begin) in 1994 when she __________ (join) one of the first all girl bands – the Spice Girls. Together the five girls __________ (sell) millions of CDs and __________ (become) famous all around the world. But about six years later, the dream suddenly __________ (end) when one of them __________ (leave) the band and the others __________ (decide) to go their own way too. Victoria __________ (be) sad at the time, but she also __________ (see) the end of the Spice Girls as a chance to follow her next dream: to become a fashion designer. At first most people __________ (not take) her seriously and they __________ (make) fun of her. But today nobody is laughing. Today she __________ (become) one of Britain's most popular designers. She __________ (win) lots of prizes and she ____________ (just open) her own clothes shop.

Green Line 3
Vorschläge zur Leistungsmessung
ISBN: 978-3-12-834234-4

5 A trip to Scotland!

Adjective or adverb? Complete Amber's diary entry with the correct forms.

We drove up to Scotland yesterday and the journey was __________ (terrible). Gwen's parents drove much too __________ (fast), but it still took hours because we got lost. Holly and Gwen chatted __________ (loud) all the way about __________ (silly) things. They are still little kids!

But then we arrived and I met Ethan!! He's great. He talked __________ (quiet) to me all evening and laughed with me while we were eating. He's so __________ (funny)!

Today I went with him to band practice. He plays the bagpipes really __________ (good) and he can sing __________ (beautiful) too. The other people in his band were really __________ (friendly) and I had a great time there. On the way back we walked __________ (slow) through the streets of Glasgow and he showed me the places he likes best.

I'm going to have a __________ (great) time here, I think.

6 Holly's e-mail from Scotland

Complete Holly's e-mail with an adjective or adverb of manner.

Dear Olivia,

We're having a __________ (fantastic) time here in Scotland. Gwen's aunt, uncle and cousin are really ____________ (nice) and they're looking after us really ___________ (good). We've seen lots of things in Glasgow. On Friday we drove to Loch Lomond and walked up a mountain called Ben Lomond. There were __________ (beautiful) views of the lake and the countryside from the top, but we didn't have time to enjoy it because we saw some black clouds which were coming in __________ (quick) from the sea. We took some __________ (funny) photos and then walked down again really __________ (fast).

Yesterday evening we went to a ceilidh. That's a kind of party where people dance together in groups. It's ___________ (great) fun. As the music gets faster, you dance ___________ (wild) round in circles. Of course I fell over after a while. Everybody laughed so __________ (hard) ☺

See you soon, Holly

Klett
Green Line 3
Vorschläge zur Leistungsmessung
ISBN: 978-3-12-834234-4

7 The Aberdeen Youth Festival

*Put in **who, which/that** or **whose**.*

Aberdeen is a large Scottish city ________ location is very practical, because it is near Edinburgh *and* Glasgow. It's a city ________ many people want to visit. A festival ________ welcomes young people from all over the world takes place every summer there.

Young dancers, actors and musicians ________ are from over eighty countries first started coming to the festival in 1973, and every year it gets bigger. This is a great possibility for young people to learn about music, theatre and dance from all around the world. It is an event ________ puts on over eighty performances in nine days, so there's a lot to see! Summer courses ________ offer classes in acting, dancing and singing are open to everyone and the students ________ go to these often put on free shows outside the main festival area. The students ________ shows are the most popular are invited back the next year. The information ________ you can find on the festival website will tell you everything you need to know for a great visit!

8 Highland life in the past

Make one sentence from two sentences using relative pronouns.

1. Before 1755, many people were farmers. They lived in the Scottish Highlands.

   ____

2. The Highlanders belonged to clans. The clans all had different names.

   ____

3. Every clan had a leader. His job was to keep the clan safe.

   ____

4. Farmers and their animals lived together in small stone houses. They were called crofts.

   ____

5. The crofts had very thick stone walls. The walls kept out the cold.

   ____

6. A very rich man wanted the farms back from the Highlanders. The farms were on his land.

   ____

7. Some farmers wanted to leave Scotland forever. They had lost their land.

   ____

Klett
Green Line 3
Vorschläge zur Leistungsmessung
ISBN: 978-3-12-834234-4

9 The race

Ben Miller participated in a 1,470 kilometre bicycle race from Lands End in the south of England to John O'Groats in the north of Scotland. He was the winner! Here is what Ben writes about this day in his blog. Complete the text with the correct past progressive forms of the verbs.

When I arrived in John O'Groats, it was very noisy and busy! People ______________ (shout) and loud music ______________ (play). Someone told me I was the winner but I ______________ (not even listen) – I was so tired, hungry and thirsty! The others ______________ (not pay attention) to me. I knew my family ______________ (wait) for me but I couldn't see them because there was so much activity. Children ______________ (run around) everywhere and people ______________ (take) photos.

Then I saw my sister. She ______________ (stand) there with a big smile on her face. And what ______________ (she – hold)? A huge burger and some water for me. I was very happy to see her!

10 An experience of life in the past

Complete the text with the simple past or past progressive form of the verbs.

Hi Julie! You know how Mum and Dad are always saying that we don't know how lucky we are and that our life in Glasgow is too easy? Well, yesterday they took us to visit a family who live on a farm in the Highlands! Their lives are nothing like ours – they don't even have electricity or water! When we ______________ (arrive), Tom and his Dad ______________ (collect) wood in the forest. We ______________ (go) to help them and then we ______________ (take) the wood back to the house where Tom's mum ______________ (wait) for us. While she ______________ (make) a fire, I ______________ (look) out of the window and saw their Dad. What ______________ (he – do)? He ______________ (try) to catch a chicken for our lunch! In the afternoon, we ______________ (take) some big buckets down to the river to get water for their showers that night! Then we ______________ (feed) all the animals. Finally, it was time to go home and, as we were leaving, I ______________ (look) back into their small, dark house. Of course, they ______________ (not watch) TV and they ______________ (not play) computer games!

It was a cool experience, but I couldn't live like that – I like my easy life too much! Love, Lucy

ISBN: 978-3-12-834234-4

11 Work in a factory in the Victorian era

Complete the thoughts of Oliver, a boy from the times of the Industrial Revolution, with the correct verb forms to make conditional clauses type 2.

My brother, Mat, is very sick. I hope he won't die. If he _____________ (not have to) work in a factory, he wouldn't be so sick. He's only ten and he has to work ten hours every day. That just isn't fair. If we were rich, he _____________ (not have to) work. Rich children go to school. I'd love to go to school, but we aren't rich. We have to work. If I ___________ (go) to school, I ____________ (be able to) read. I'm thirteen and I work in a rich lady's house. They have hundreds of books. If I ____________ (can) read, I _____________ (be able to) find out about lots of things. Maybe I'd be able to find out how to make Mat better.

Of course, it isn't all that easy. If we ___________ (not have) a job, we probably _____________ (not have) enough to eat. And if we didn't have enough to eat, we ___________ (all – be) sick.

12 The thoughts of Queen Elizabeth I

Use the verbs to make conditional clauses type 2. Start your sentence with the first word given.

1. If – I – marry – my husband – try – to rule – the country.

   I must not marry! ____

2. What – I – do – in the evening – if – I – can – not – watch – Shakespeare's plays?

   ____

3. I – not enjoy – going to the Globe – so much – if – his plays – not be – so fantastic.

   ____

4. England – not – be – so rich – if – Drake – not be – so clever.

   ____

5. If – our sailors – not be – so good – we – not be able to – start colonies in America – now.

   ____

6. If – I – not be – Queen – life – be – very different – for me.

   ____

Klett
Green Line 3
Vorschläge zur Leistungsmessung
ISBN: 978-3-12-834234-4

Unit 1 Find your place

Allgemeine Hinweise zur Bewertung von offenen Schreibaufgaben

Die insgesamt zu vergebende Punktzahl für offene Schreibaufgaben setzt sich aus den Bereichen inhaltliche Leistung (Orientierung an der Aufgabenstellung, Umfang, Textsorte, Textaufbau) und sprachliche Leistung (Sprache, Wortschatz, Strukturen, Orthographie) zusammen.

Allgemeine Hinweise zur Bewertung von offenen Sprachmittlungsaufgaben

Die insgesamt zu vergebende Punktzahl für offene Sprachmittlungsaufgaben setzt sich aus den Bereichen inhaltliche Leistung (Orientierung an der Aufgabenstellung / Bezug auf situativen Kontext, sinngemäße sowie situations- und adressatenbezogene Wiedergabe der Informationen) und sprachliche Leistung (eigenständige Formulierung, Wortschatz, Satzbau, Strukturen, Orthographie) zusammen.

1 Listening: I need some advice!

Either (→ 6 Punkte)
1. because they're fun 2. He hates losing at sport. 3. She thinks it was awful. 4. He writes great stories.
5. He helped Holly in IT 6. to become a vet

Or (→ 12 Punkte)
a) + b) 1. true 2. false (She knows what they say isn't always true.) 3. false (Holly agrees that Luke is competitive.) 4. false (Luke says he's really bad at making things.) 5. true 6. true 7. true 8. false (It's Holly's dream to be a vet in the future.)

2 Listening: Can we compromise?

Either (→ 6 Punkte)
1. c 2. b 3. a 4. c 5. b 6. c

Or (→ 8 Punkte)
match; stay at home; Science project; two matches; my uncle; one hour; get up; my homework

3 Reading: How to be confident

Either
a) 1. B 2. D 3. E 4. A 5. — 6. C 7. F (→ 6 Punkte)
b) *Individuelle S-Antwort* (→ 2 Punkte)

Or (→ 6 Punkte)
1. B 2. D 3. F 4. C 5. A 6. E

4 Reading: I want to be famous!

Either (→ 6 Punkte)
1. his life is boring 2. to be a big star 3. he's good at 4. enjoy himself with his friends 5. like everyone else 6. what his dream is

Or (→ 8 Punkte)
1. life is boring 2. make a difference 3. They want to be a big star. 4. Choose something you're good at. 5. Work hard. 6. Practise a lot. 7. Show you're different. 8. Don't forget your dream. / Don't give up.

5 Writing: Advice please!

Lösungsvorschlag:

Hi Ella,
I'm really happy that your sister's hockey team is in the finals. That's great! I'm sure she's very excited and of course she wants her friends and family to watch the match, so I don't agree with your compromise. I know you love tennis and that your match is important too, but it isn't a final. I think Ruby would be very upset if you didn't go to watch her and she needs to see you in the crowd! In your situation, I would go and watch Ruby. I hope that helps!

Inhaltliche Leistung:	→ 6 Punkte
Sprachliche Leistung:	→ 4 Punkte
Gesamtpunktzahl:	→ 10 Punkte

Green Line 3
Vorschläge zur Leistungsmessung
ISBN: 978-3-12-834234-4

6 Writing: The big match

Lösungsvorschlag:

"Come on Ruby!" shouted the other girls in her team. "You're dreaming!" They were right – she should stop thinking about Ella and try really hard for the last three minutes. She ran forward, took the ball from a girl in the other team, then hit it very hard. "Goal!" everyone shouted. Ruby's team were the winners and Ruby was the star of the match … but she was still angry with her sister. Then, suddenly, she heard her sister's voice. "Not bad, Ruby!" She turned and Ella was smiling at her. "Where were you?" Ruby asked. Ella showed Ruby her phone. "I was behind the goal – look, I took some fantastic photos of your goals!" Sometimes, Ruby loved her sister!

Inhaltliche Leistung: → 6 Punkte
Sprachliche Leistung: → 4 Punkte
Gesamtpunktzahl: → 10 Punkte

7 Mediation: I've had an idea!

Lösungsvorschlag:

Hi! My aunt has had a good idea – she thinks you could help her children with their English while you are staying with me. She would be very happy if you spent an hour or two every day playing with the children and speaking to them in English – but it doesn't matter if you can't go every day. She will pay you, of course, and it would be really good experience if you wanted to work with children in the future. What do you think?

Inhaltliche Leistung: → 6 Punkte
Sprachliche Leistung: → 4 Punkte
Gesamtpunktzahl: → 10 Punkte

8 Mediation: An animal photo competition

Lösungsvorschlag:

Hi! Ich habe gerade online etwas über einen Tierfoto-Wettbewerb gelesen. Da habe ich an dich gedacht, weil du tolle Fotos von Tieren machst! Du musst ein kreatives Foto schicken, das du selbst geschossen hast und du musst es mit einer Beschreibung, wo und wann du es gemacht hast vor dem 4. November einschicken. Wenn du den ersten Preis gewinnen würdest, würdest du 1000 Pfund bekommen! Der zweite Preis ist eine Kamera. Ich finde, du solltest teilnehmen!

Inhaltliche Leistung: → 5 Punkte
Sprachliche Leistung: → 3 Punkte
Gesamtpunktzahl: → 8 Punkte

9 Vocabulary: Adjectives (→ 8 Punkte)

1. successful/famous 2. rich 3. stressed out 4. laid back 5. confident 6. creative/imaginative 7. competitive 8. smart

10 Vocabulary: Life isn't fair! (→ 8 Punkte)

push myself; in your shoes; enjoy myself; the way I am; messy; bossy; in charge; behave

11 Language: My dream (→ 10 Punkte)

'd be; won; had; would enter; didn't win; would help; wouldn't sleep; bought; happened; would be

12 Language: If things were different … (→ 12 Punkte)

1. If I was/were in town on Saturday, I would enter the competition.
2. If Anna liked cooking, she would make a birthday cake.
3. If Tom enjoyed dancing or singing, he would take part in the talent show.
4. If we lived near a park, we would play sport more often.
5. If they liked to travel, they would go to London.
6. If Ben had a talent for Maths, he would like Maths lessons.

13 Language: The talent show (→ 12 Punkte)

1. If I danced like him, I'd/would leave school tomorrow!
2. If you don't stop dreaming, you'll/will fail your exams!
3. I'd/would look cool too if my hair was longer!

Green Line 3
Vorschläge zur Leistungsmessung
ISBN: 978-3-12-834234-4

4. If she knew how to do it, she'd/would be a famous designer!
5. I'd/would be happy to join them if they asked me!
6. If I could have singing lessons, I'd/would be able to enter next year's show!

14 Language: Your own ideas (→ 8 Punkte)

Lösungsvorschlag:

1. If I have time next weekend, I will visit my grandma.
2. If I could choose a special talent, I would want to be a really good singer.
3. If I didn't have to go to school, I would sleep late every day!
4. If I decide to celebrate my next birthday, I will have a theme party.

15 Language: Let's talk about ourselves! (→ 7 Punkte)

1. himself 2. ourselves 3. myself 4. yourselves 5. yourself 6. themselves 7. herself

16 Language: Saturday sports camp (→ 9 Punkte)

ourselves; myself; each other; yourself/yourselves; each other; each other; yourselves; each other; yourselves

Text smart 1 Poems and songs

"Another view"

1 Comprehension

a) 1. C 2. E 3. G 4. F 5. A 6. B 7. D (→ 7 Punkte)
b) 1. false 2. false 3. true 4. true 5. false 6. false (→ 6 Punkte)

2 Structure and meaning

a) *Erwartungshorizont* (→ 4 Punkte)
The speaker is a boy who is hiking in the countryside with his father. He is unhappy because he doesn't like the countryside. His dad thinks the surroundings are beautiful, but he doesn't agree with him.
b) *Erwartungshorizont* (→ 4 Punkte)
The rhyme scheme is ABCB in every verse. The speaker repeats the last line of each verse in the first line of the next verse.

"Grandpa"

1 Comprehension (→ 4 Punkte)

1. b) 2. a) 3. c) 4. a)

2 Structure and meaning

a) There is no rhyme scheme. (→ 2 Punkte)
b) *Lösungsvorschlag:* (→ 4 Punkte)
1. calm/peaceful/friendly 2. sad; it makes me think of my grandpa who died 3. good/warm/loving
c) *Individuelle S-Antwort*

Inhaltliche Leistung:	→ 6 Punkte
Sprachliche Leistung:	→ 4 Punkte
Gesamtpunktzahl:	→ 10 Punkte

Green Line 3
Vorschläge zur Leistungsmessung
ISBN: 978-3-12-834234-4

3 Comparing two poems

a) *Erwartungshorizont:* (→ 8 Punkte)

	"Another view"	"Grandpa"
Form	regular; short lines and sentences; last line of each verse is first line of next verse	irregular, 2 long lines, 2 short lines, words aren't repeated
Length	5 verses	Just one verse
Rhyme scheme	ABCB	No real/strong rhymes
Topic	the same for both poems: two people from one family; one is young, one is old, but the mood in "Another view" is unhappy, the mood in "Grandpa" is friendly/happy	

b) *Erwartungshorizont:* (→ 6 Punkte)
"Grandpa": The speaker is interested in Grandpa and his secrets/his past. They seem to have a good relationship.
"Another view": The speaker is not interested in his dad's "old" world. They don't seem to have a very close relationship. The speaker's father is getting on his son's nerves.

Unit 2 Let's go to Scotland!

1 Listening: Best of friends?

Either (→ 13 Punkte)
a) + b) 1. false (Alfie says Sofia doesn't need both of them.) 2. false (They didn't plan to meet her. They just saw her on the street.) 3. true 4. false (Sofia is from London.) 5. false (Sofia likes to play hockey.) 6. true 7. true 8. false (Sofia wants to bring Jack to the gig.)

Or
a) 3 (→ 3 Punkte)
b) (→ 10 Punkte)
Sofia: 1, 6, 8, 9, 10 Sofia's mum: 4 (, 7) Callum: 5, 6, 7, 9 Alfie: 2, 3, 4, 7

2 Listening: It always rains …

Either (→ 10 Punkte)
1. b 2. a 3. b, c 4. a, c 5. a, b 6. a, b

Or (→ 10 Punkte)

Country	**Cliché**
Germany	1. Germans don't have a sense of humour. 2. Germans are always on time. 3. Girls are called Gretel. 4. Germans work hard.
England	5. The weather isn't great. It rains a lot. 6. The English like to stand in queues. 7. The English like to talk about the weather.
Scotland	8. Scottish people want to save as much money as possible. 9. The Scots drink whisky. 10. Scottish people wear kilts all day.

Klett
Green Line 3
Vorschläge zur Leistungsmessung
ISBN: 978-3-12-834234-4

3 Reading: Scotland's islands

Either (→ 9 Punkte)
Skye: 1, 2, 3, 4, 6
Orkney: 1, 2, 4, 5

Or (→ 12 Punkte)

	Skye	Orkney
Geography / Nature	one island; hills; beautiful countryside; birds and other wildlife	70 islands; spectacular cliffs / hills / coastline; fascinating wildlife
History	people have lived here for thousands of years	stone age villages; Skara Brae
Culture	3,000 Gaelic speakers, Aros centre, castles	art, music

4 Reading: Was that Robert the Bruce?

Either (→ 7 Punkte)
1. false 2. false 3. true 4. false 5. true 6. false 7. true

Or (→ 6 Punkte)
1. when Robbie was three 2. (alone) on the farm in Scotland 3. they aren't safe 4. to move to England 5. to climb to the roof 6. saved his sister

5 Writing: St Andrews

Lösungsvorschlag:
You're looking for the perfect place to stay in Scotland? You want everything: nice people, beautiful beaches, historic town and spectacular views? Not possible, you say? Come to St Andrews and think again! St Andrews is lucky in its almost perfect location. It's on the coast, but not far from hills or from Dundee. It's one of the oldest cities in Scotland. It was first written about in the 7th century and has been important historically since then. Although it's a small town, there's so much to do here. You can walk around and just enjoy the views and the friendly people or you can visit one of the many historical buildings, take a walk along the beach or of course, play golf. Do you want to tour several places in Scotland? Then don't start in St Andrews because you may not want to leave!

Inhaltliche Leistung: → 5 Punkte
Sprachliche Leistung: → 5 Punkte
Gesamtpunktzahl: → 10 Punkte

6 Writing: An accident!

a) *Lösungsvorschlag*

Father: Isn't it beautiful here? Look at this landscape!
Jack: Yeah, it's OK …
Katie: I think the hills and lakes are very pretty, Dad!
Father: Yes, you're right.
Jack: Hey, Katie, look over there! You won't believe it!
Katie: What? What is it? Oh, wow! Hey, Dad, there's Nessie!
Father: Oh, you two … You know there isn't really a monster in Loch Ness.
Jack: But Dad, there it is, look!
Father: Oh, alright … hey, what is that? No, that can't be!
Katie: Aaah! Dad, you're driving into the sheep, be careful!
Father: Oh, thank you, Katie. That was really close!
Katie: Oh no, I think Nessie is gone now …

Inhaltliche Leistung: → 5 Punkte
Sprachliche Leistung: → 3 Punkte
Gesamtpunktzahl: → 8 Punkte

b) *Individuelle S-Antwort*
Inhaltliche Leistung: → 6 Punkte
Sprachliche Leistung: → 3 Punkte
Gesamtpunktzahl: → 9 Punkte

Green Line 3
Vorschläge zur Leistungsmessung
ISBN: 978-3-12-834234-4

7 Mediation: A visit to Innsbruck

a) (→ 8 Punkte)

Ellis: What is the picture? Is that a ski jump?
You: Yes, it's the Bergisel ski jump. You get a good view of the town from there. (→ 1 Punkt)
Yvonne: What's that about the Steinzeit? Was the city built in the Stone Age?
You: No, it says that people have lived here since the Stone Age. The city was founded in 1180. (→ 1 Punkt)
Ellis: What can you do in Innsbruck?
You: You can visit the historical city centre and see the sights or just enjoy it here. (→ 2 Punkte)
Yvonne: But I don't want to stay in the city all the time. Can you do anything else?
You: Yes, you can go climbing and walking in the mountains. There are some spectacular views there. (→ 2 Punkte)
Chris: That sounds good. Are the mountains near the city?
You: Yes, they're very near to the north and south. (→ 1 Punkt)
Yvonne: It says something about riding too. Can you go riding near here? Even beginners?
You: Yes, you can go riding there, even if you can't ride well. (→ 1 Punkt)

b) Innsbruck is great for sightseeing. In the old town you can see the "Goldene Dachl" and enjoy the historic and lively atmosphere. From the "Bergiselschanze" you get a great view over the town. All around Innsbruck there's nature and mountains. I know you'd like to do some activities too. Just outside Innsbruck you can go climbing, horse riding, mountain biking or trekking.

Inhaltliche Leistung: → 5 Punkte
Sprachliche Leistung: → 4 Punkte
Gesamtpunktzahl: → 9 Punkte

8 Vocabulary: Scotland's choice (→ 13 Punkte)

referendum; independence; kilts; thistles; queue; bagpipes; backpack; tartan; flags; parties; band; anthem; national

9 Vocabulary: A puzzle

a) (→ 16 Punkte)
1. shipbuilding 2. ban 3. discovery 4. scientist 5. invent 6. sauce 7. crane 8. steam 9. musical 10. vegetarian 11. Scot 12. narrow 13. vegetables 14. meat 15. mashed 16. raincoat

b) *Lösungsvorschlag:* (→ 7 Punkte)
subject: another word for 'topic'
fill: put something into something else, for example juice into a glass
set off: start going somewhere
penicillin: something that can help you when you are very sick
midnight: twelve o'clock at night
a close: something narrow you can go through
hundreds (of): a big number of / more than 200

10 Language: Who's been writing to you? (→ 9 Punkte)

Have you been having; 've been enjoying; since; Has she been making; 's been talking; for; 's been thinking; since; hasn't been getting

11 Language: What do you know about Holly? (→ 12 Punkte)

1. Holly has been going to Thomas Tallis School since she was eleven.
2. Holly and Olivia have been sitting next to each other in classes since their first day at TTS.
3. Holly hasn't been wearing pink for a few months.
4. Holly and Amber have been living alone with their mum since their dad moved out.
5. Holly hasn't been eating meat since she was ten.
6. Holly and Amber have been staying in Scotland for about a week.

12 Language: Rescued from Ben Lomond! (→ 12 Punkte)

Last Sunday two young tourists were rescued by the Lomond Mountain Rescue Team.
This is known by climbers with experience, but this fact is often not known or even ignored by tourists.
A search for the missing teens was started by the mountain rescue team right away.

Green Line 3
Vorschläge zur Leistungsmessung
ISBN: 978-3-12-834234-4

They were found at half past three.
They were taken to hospital by the rescue people.
They have been told to be more careful next time.

13 Language: Nessie! (→ 9 Punkte)

were told; were taken; is known; has been seen; have been taken; has been searched; has been found; are found; are given

14 Viewing: The Scottish referendum

a) + b) (→ 11 Punkte)
1. false (The referendum started at 7 o'clock in the morning.) 2. false (The reporter said that Scotland had a long and proud history.) 3. false (Before the referendum there was a two-year campaign.) 4. true 5. false (They flew up the west part of the country.) 6. true 7. true

c) 1. a), d), e) 2. a), e) 3. b), e) 4. c), d) 5. d), e) (→ 11 Punkte)

Text smart 2 Factual texts

"Hunters"

1 Understanding the text

a) 2. (→ 2 Punkte)
b) (→ 10 Punkte)
1. the killing caused worldwide horror (l. 7)
2. Palmer had to go into hiding. (ll 7–8)
3. a lot of people didn't know what was going on (l. 13)
4. hunters have to have special permits, which mean they can kill certain animals (l. 15)
5. Some people argue that there is a good side to the hunting. (l. 16)

2 Elements of a news report

a) give the main facts / a summary (→ 3 Punkte)
b) (→ 3 Punkte)
passive constructions in the text:
is believed to have paid (l. 5); is said to be (l. 10); was killed (l. 13); can be used (ll 16–17)

"The Countryside Code"

1 Understanding the text

a) (→ 3 Punkte)
1: Look after nature.
2: Have fun but think about what you do.
3: Follow the rules and think about others' interests.

b) 1. b) 2. a) 3. c) 4. e) 5. d) (→ 5 Punkte)

2 Compare the two factual texts (→ 9 Punkte)

steps | tells what happened | focuses on facts | several headings | sentences begin with verb | written in present tense | written almost all in past tense | report | instructions

3 Using language

a) *Erwartungshorizont:* (→ 2 Punkte)
help people; tell people what to do / how to behave
b) (→ 6 Punkte)
protect (l. 1); leave (l. 2); keep (l. 3); enjoy (l. 4); plan, be prepared (l. 5); follow (l. 6); consider (l. 7); respect, don't block (l. 8); slow down, stop (l. 10); give (l. 11)
c) to help people understand the rule (→ 1 Punkt)

Green Line 3
Vorschläge zur Leistungsmessung
ISBN: 978-3-12-834234-4

Unit 3 What was it like?

1 Listening: Who were they?

Either (→ 5 Punkte)
Elizabeth I: Speaker 4
A Roman: Speaker 5
A Celtic man: Speaker 2
Queen Victoria: —
Henry VIII: Speaker 1
A Norman: Speaker 3

Or (→ 6 Punkte)
1. He founded them. 2. in tribes 3. a king or queen 4. The Normans built it. / It is a Norman castle. 5. She was already married to England. 6. the calendar

2 Listening: A class trip to the Globe

Either (→ 6 Punkte)
1. next Tuesday 2. at the station 3. at 9:15 4. (guided) tour of the Globe 5. watch Romeo and Juliet / a play 6. warm clothes

Or (→ 10 Punkte)
1. a 2. a 3. a, c 4. b, c 5. a 6. a, b, c

3 Reading: The Industrial Revolution

Either (→ 8 Punkte)
1. in 1750 2. lived 3. in the countryside 4. their jobs 5. new work in the factories 6. live in towns and cities 7. very little money 8. had to go to school

Or (→ 8 Punkte)
1. d) 2. g) 3. a) 4. f) 5. b) 6. h) 7. c) 8. e)

4 Reading: Claire's e-mail to Amy

Either (→ 6 Punkte)
1. made a phone call 2. the Norman boots 3. for their smartphones 4. He was hit by an arrow. 5. The main door was locked. 6. He was having a bath.

Or (→ 9 Punkte)
a) + b) 1. false (She was late for her meeting because she'd had to make a phone call.) 2. true 3. true 4. false (He wasn't badly hurt, but he screamed when he saw blood on his hand.) 5. true 6. false (They had to wait for him for more than half an hour.)

5 Writing: A person from history

Lösungsvorschlag:
William Shakespeare was born in Stratford-upon-Avon, England in 1564. His father was a glove-maker and his mother came from a rich farming family. Few details are known about his early life, but at school he was interested in reading and writing. When he was 18 years old, he married Anne Hathaway and together they had three children. Later, Shakespeare moved to London because he wanted to become an actor. But he became famous as a writer. His plays were so popular that even Elizabeth I, and later King James, often watched them. Shakespeare died in 1616 at the age of 52.

Inhaltliche Leistung: → 6 Punkte
Sprachliche Leistung: → 4 Punkte
Gesamtpunktzahl: → 10 Punkte

6 Writing: An interview

a) *Individuelle S-Antwort*
Inhaltliche Leistung: → 5 Punkte
Sprachliche Leistung: → 6 Punkte
Gesamtpunktzahl: → 11 Punkte

b) *Individuelle S-Antwort*
Inhaltliche Leistung: → 6 Punkte
Sprachliche Leistung: → 6 Punkte
Gesamtpunktzahl: → 12 Punkte

7 Mediation: The Tower of London

Either (→ 8 Punkte)
Anne: What did the people who wrote this review think about their visit to the Tower?

Green Line 3
Vorschläge zur Leistungsmessung
ISBN: 978-3-12-834234-4

You	They enjoyed it. They say it was the highlight of their trip because they learned so much about the history of England. (→ 2 Punkte)
Anne:	I can see the words 'Beefeater Tour'. What did they say about it?
You:	They say that it was very funny and it was easy to understand too (even for people who don't speak English very well). (→ 2 Punkte)
Anne:	Was there anything they didn't like about the tour?
You:	Yes, they say it was quite expensive. (→ 1 Punkt)
Anne:	Do you think from what you've read that they'd take part in the tour again?
You:	Yes, I think they would take part again. They write that next time they'll buy their tickets online. And they'll get there early before it gets too full. (→ 3 Punkte)

Or

Lösungsvorschlag:

They say it was a highlight of their trip to London and they learned a lot about the history of England. They thought the Beefeater Tour was very funny and it was easy to understand, even for people who don't speak English very well. They had a great day. But it was quite expensive. Next time they will buy their tickets online and they will get there early before it gets too full.

Inhaltliche Leistung:	→ 5 Punkte
Sprachliche Leistung:	→ 3 Punkte
Gesamtpunktzahl:	→ 8 Punkte

8 Vocabulary: Find the words (→ 8 Punkte)

mirror; axe; necklace; sandals; calendar; boots; hairbrush; belt

9 Vocabulary: Find the missing word (→ 5 Punkte)

1. daughter 2. play 3. less 4. Spanish 5. emperor

10 Vocabulary: Words with the same meaning (→ 6 Punkte)

1. monarch 2. to start 3. noisy 4. to marry 5. back then 6. to grow

11 Vocabulary: Definitions

a) (→ 7 Punkte)
   1. battle 2. slave 3. to grow up 4. bracelet 5. crown 6. education 7. What was it like?

b) *Lösungsvorschlag:* (→ 5 Punkte)
   favourite: the thing you like best; stage: the place in a theatre where the actors are;
   writer: a person who writes theatre plays or books;
   to experience: When you experience something, it happens to you.;
   to change one's mind: to think about something again so you have a different opinion about it

12 Vocabulary: A Beefeater tour (→ 10 Punkte)

dates back to; was built; reign; is made of; brought over; built; blood; murder; What luck; forward

13 Language: Elizabeth I (→ 14 Punkte)

became; had died; celebrated; were; had ruled; hadn't been; enjoyed; was; sailed; hadn't been; brought; had stolen; died; had become

14 Language: The Man in Grey (→ 21 Punkte)

had; had (Claire) done; 'd given; had invited; was; 'd never been; got; went; sat down; noticed; looked; had to; wanted; looked; had gone; told; had happened; saw; said; asked; laughed

15 Language: If they hadn't … (→ 10 Punkte)

1. If Olivia and Holly hadn't been interested in Elizabeth I, they wouldn't have joined the Tudor group.
2. If Holly hadn't been late for the photo shoot, Olivia wouldn't have begun to get nervous.
3. If Olivia hadn't had two ladies-in-waiting, she wouldn't have looked important.
4. If Holly hadn't fallen off her skates on the way, she wouldn't have been late.
5. If she hadn't broken her arm, she wouldn't have had to wear a plaster cast for the photo.

Green Line 3
Vorschläge zur Leistungsmessung
ISBN: 978-3-12-834234-4

16 Language: Jay is grounded again … (→ 13 Punkte)

would never have found out; hadn't told; hadn't found out; wouldn't have been; would have said; had asked; hadn't told; would never have happened; had worked; would have got; had got; wouldn't have been; could have gone

17 Viewing: Shakespeare and the Globe

a) 1., 2., 4., 6. (→ 4 Punkte)
b) 1. c) 2. a), c) 3. a), b), c) 4. a), c) 5. c) 6. b) 7. a), b) 8. c) (→ 13 Punkte)
c) (→ 2 Punkte)
The speaker uses the present tense so that the viewers can feel what it was like back then.

Text smart 3 Fictional texts

1 Understanding the text

a) 1. stomach 2. silence 3. darkness 4. stepping 5. missing (→ 5 Punkte)
b) 3, 7, 4, 2, 6, 1, 5 (→ 7 Punkte)
c) *Erwartungshorizont:* (→ 4 Punkte)
- He lives with his mum.
- His dad lives in America and they don't talk to each other very often.
- He's 13 years old.
- He's been having the same nightmare for a while.

2 Elements of a fictional text

1. The narrative perspective
a) third person narrator; Conor's perspective (→ 2 Punkte)
b) *Lösungsvorschlag:* (→ 3 Punkte)
If the text was written from the perspective of Conor's mum, for example, she would be in a different room of the house, so maybe she wouldn't hear the same scary things he hears.
Then she probably wouldn't be as scared as he is.

2. The senses
a) hear (→ 2 Punkte)
b) (→ 4 Punkte)
see: He looked over at the clock (l. 15); Conor blinked sleepily (l. 26); He didn't want to … look more than anything. (ll 68–70); **feel:** He felt a sudden panic, his stomach twisting. (l. 41)

3. Suspense
a) (→ 6 Punkte)
things we don't understand yet; something surprising and scary; reader shares a character's fear; descriptions with lots of detail; ending at a dramatic moment; important word repeated
b) *Individuelle S-Antwort*

Inhaltliche Leistung:	→ 5 Punkte
Sprachliche Leistung:	→ 3 Punkte
Gesamtpunktzahl:	→ 8 Punkte

Unit 4 On the move

1 Listening: At the airport

Either (→ 5 Punkte)
3, —, 2, 5, 1, 4

Or (→ 12 Punkte)
a) + b) 1. false (The passengers may use mobile phones in the flight setting.) 2. true 3. false (Boarding will start in a minute.) 4. true 5. false (The passengers are asked to wait in the departure lounge.) 6. true 7. false (Boarding is at quarter past ten from gate 42.) 8. true

Green Line 3
Vorschläge zur Leistungsmessung
ISBN: 978-3-12-834234-4

2 Listening: "True" stories

Either

a) B, A, E, D (→ 4 Punkte)

b) (→ 4 Punkte)

C: It was the pilot who was outside the door.

F: It was the pilot who was scared of flying.

Or (→ 12 Punkte)

1. One plane couldn't land because of the bad weather. → three planes
2. One plane had to land because the pilot was ill. → scared
3. One pilot asked the passengers to push the plane to the terminal. → away from the building
4. Usually airport workers push the plane away from the building. → a special car pushes
5. A plane couldn't leave once because a passenger was still outside. → the pilot
6. A passenger was asked to sit on the toilet because he was ill. → the plane was full

3 Reading: Friends for life?

Either (→ 6 Punkte)

1. horses and sport 2. in Munich 3. disappointed 4. talk to them about it politely 5. good / they understood 6. be more honest and less polite

Or (→ 8 Punkte)

When?	How did Gemma feel?	Why?
Before the trip	excited	her exchange partner sounded nice / Munich sounded great / she loves foreign languages
At the end of the first day	disappointed	the family spoke in English
On Sunday evening	embarrassed	she had to say she wasn't happy about something
Two weeks later	happy and sad	happy because the trip was great and sad because she had to leave

4 Reading: A new life

Either (→ 7 Punkte)

5, 4, 7, 3, 1, 6, 2

Or (→ 12 Punkte)

2. 7–8: "he knew … country." 3. 13–14: "He was … still is." 4. 14–16: "One year … get away." 5. 23–25: "He became … chairs." 6. 25–27: "An English teacher … ticket." 7. 32–33: "Dad was … England …"

5 Writing: It's fun to travel

Lösungsvorschlag Bild 1:

Man: I'm so scared, I can't do this! I want to get out!
Flight attendant: Don't worry, everything is going to be OK. You're completely safe. Please try to calm down.
Man: But the weather outside is really bad, look!
Flight attendant: Don't worry, we often fly in bad weather and nothing has ever happened. Would you like to have a glass of water?
Man: Well, OK … thank you.

Lösungsvorschlag Bild 2:

Man: Excuse me, I was on flight AF 7655. When I wanted to collect my luggage, it wasn't there!
Airport worker: Are you sure? Maybe you just need to wait a little longer.
Man: I've been waiting for half an hour!
Airport worker: Oh, OK. It should be there by now … Would you please fill in this form so we can help you find your luggage?
Man: Hmm, well . . OK then.

Inhaltliche Leistung: → 5 Punkte
Sprachliche Leistung: → 3 Punkte
Gesamtpunktzahl: → 8 Punkte

Klett
Green Line 3
Vorschläge zur Leistungsmessung
ISBN: 978-3-12-834234-4

6 Writing: A travel report

a) *Individuelle S-Antwort*

Inhaltliche Leistung: → 6 Punkte
Sprachliche Leistung: → 4 Punkte
Gesamtpunktzahl: → 10 Punkte

b) *Individuelle S-Antwort*

Inhaltliche Leistung: → 6 Punkte
Sprachliche Leistung: → 4 Punkte
Gesamtpunktzahl: → 10 Punkte

7 Mediation: What did she say? (→ 8 Punkte)

Jean: Where is Lea now?
You: She's still waiting at the airport. (→ 1 Punkt)
Jean: Why? What happened?
You: There was something wrong with the plane. (→ 1 Punkt)
Jean: Oh no. But did everything else go well?
You: No, at first she had problems at passport control. Then she had a problem going through security control. She was late after that and had to run to the gate. (→ 3 Punkte)
Jean: What is she doing now?
You: She's waiting in the departure lounge. (→ 1 Punkt)
Jean: Ohhhh …
You: But she says that this is OK. And she told me to say thank you for the lemonade. It tasted very good. (→ 2 Punkte)

8 Vocabulary: At the airport (→ 8 Punkte)

1. luggage 2. boarding card 3. passport 4. duty-free shop 5. flight attendant 6. passengers 7. plane 8. suitcase

9 Vocabulary: What's the word?

a) 1. e) 2. h) 3. g) 4. b) 5. c) 6. a) 7. f) 8. d) (→ 8 Punkte)
b) (→ 3 Punkte)
soup: a meal you eat with a spoon
hostel: You can sleep there when you are on a trip and it's cheaper than a hotel.
mutter: talk quietly so that people can't understand what you're saying very well

10 Vocabulary: Word pairs (→ 8 Punkte)

1. ≠ arrivals 2. ≠ truth 3. = search for 4. ≠ security 5. ≠ get in 6. ≠ out of 7. = purpose 8. ≠ take-off

11 Language: A trip by train! (→ 7 Punkte)

1. he was still waiting for the train 2. would help her with her suitcases 3. couldn't have any chips; had just eaten three sandwiches 4. had wanted to build trains when he had been a child 5. she would call 6. he was very sorry but that he hadn't seen him

12 Language: Lucy's class goes to France (→ 9 Punkte)

there that evening; the next day; that day; take; she; the next day; the day before; there; the following week

13 Language: At the end of the trip (→ 10 Punkte)

He/She asked if we had all had a good time. He/She asked what we had liked best. Luke asked when we would arrive home. He/She asked if we were all happy we were going home. Luke asked if we had to pack out things then.

14 Language: On the ferry (→ 5 Punkte)

1. not to run 2. to listen to the security instructions 3. not to throw any rubbish in the sea 4. to help her with her bags 5. to go to their cars then

Green Line 3
Vorschläge zur Leistungsmessung
ISBN: 978-3-12-834234-4

15 Language: The French exchange (→ 13 Punkte)

was having; had eaten; what she had eaten; 'd/had had; the day before; if I knew; drank; not to drink; was sure; would call; couldn't call; was going; not to stay out

Text smart 4 Drama

1 Understanding the text

a) (→ 5 Punkte)
   1. given your all 2. just about 3. get this straight 4. make up your mind 5. shut up

b) (→ 6 Punkte)
   1. a big match 2. the players for the team 3. play in the match / be on the team 4. he has a music exam 5. between the exam and the team 6. why there's so much trouble about a football match

2 Elements of a dramatic text

a) 1. a) 2. e) 3. b) 4. c) 5. b), d) 6. e) (→ 6 Punkte)

b) *Individuelle S-Antwort*

Inhaltliche Leistung:	→ 5 Punkte
Sprachliche Leistung:	→ 3 Punkte
Gesamtpunktzahl:	→ 8 Punkte

Revision

Conditional clauses type 1

1 The French exam (→ 14 Punkte)

work; 'll do; 'll help; learn; look at; do; won't give; work; 'll make; 'm not able to; 'll get; copy; copies; 'll be

2 What will happen to me if you leave, Shahid? (→ 13 Punkte)

get; 'll stay; offers; 'll have to; happens; 'll be; 'll go; move away; 'll still have; won't have; 'm grounded; follow; won't be grounded

Simple past vs. present perfect

3 Stars UK (→ 12 Punkte)

threw; went; found out; has already worked; has already sung; sang; were; wrote; 've/have been; haven't watched; asked; 've/have had

4 The life of the fashion designer Victoria Beckham (→ 19 Punkte)

has been; has had; has always worked; has never given up; has always believed; began; joined; sold; became; ended; left; decided; was; saw; didn't take; made; has become; has won; has just opened

Adverbs of manner

5 A trip to Scotland! (→ 11 Punkte)

terrible; fast; loudly; silly; quietly; funny; well; beautifully; friendly; slowly; great

6 Holly's e-mail from Scotland (→ 10 Punkte)

fantastic; nice; well; beautiful; quickly; funny; fast; great; wildly; hard

Klett
Green Line 3
Vorschläge zur Leistungsmessung
ISBN: 978-3-12-834234-4

Defining relative clauses

7 The Aberdeen Youth Festival (→ 9 Punkte)

whose; which/that; which/that; who; which/that; which/that; who; whose; which/that

8 Highland life in the past (→ 14 Punkte)

1. Before 1755, many people who lived in the Scottish Highlands were farmers.
2. The Highlanders belonged to clans which/that all had different names.
3. Every clan had a leader whose job was to keep the clan safe.
4. Farmers and their animals lived together in small stone houses which/that were called crofts.
5. The crofts had very thick stone walls which/that kept out the cold.
6. A very rich man wanted the farms which/that were on his land back from the Highlanders.
7. Some farmers who had lost their land wanted to leave Scotland forever.

Past progressive

9 The race (→ 9 Punkte)

were shouting; was playing; wasn't even listening; weren't paying attention; was waiting; were running around; were taking; was standing; was she holding

10 An experience of life in the past (→ 14 Punkte)

arrived; were collecting; went; took; was waiting; was making; looked; was he doing; was trying; took; fed; looked; weren't watching; weren't playing

Conditional clauses type 2

11 Work in a factory in the Victorian era (→ 9 Punkte)

didn't have to; wouldn't have to; went: 'd/would be able to; could; 'd/would be able to; didn't have; wouldn't have; 'd/would all be

12 The thoughts of Queen Elizabeth I (→ 12 Punkte)

1. If I married, my husband would try to rule the country.
2. What would I do in the evening if I couldn't watch Shakespeare's plays?
3. I wouldn't enjoy going to the Globe so much if his plays weren't so fantastic.
4. England wouldn't be so rich if Drake wasn't/weren't so clever.
5. If our sailors weren't so good, we wouldn't be able to start colonies in America now.
6. If I weren't/wasn't Queen, life would be very different for me.

Klett
Green Line 3
Vorschläge zur Leistungsmessung
ISBN: 978-3-12-834234-4

Unit 1

Warm up:
- Have you ever had an embarrassing situation at school or in a club? Describe it.
- Have you ever had to make a difficult decision? How did you decide what to do?

Monologues: Model answers

A1 There's a basketball match and there are two minutes and ten seconds left to play. The score is 80-69 and the guest team is winning. The players from the home team look nervous and sad. The coach is talking to them. He looks angry and he's waving his arms excitedly. One of the players is telling him something. Maybe she's explaining what has gone wrong.

A2 A group of boys and girls are dancing. The older students are teaching the younger ones the dance moves. A boy and a girl are having problems with the moves. They look very confused. Some of the other students are laughing at them. The older students are helping and telling the others to stop laughing.

B1 A boy and a girl are standing on a stage in front of an audience of other students. They are acting a scene, but the boy has forgotten his text. He looks very nervous and scared. The girl looks embarrassed. Maybe she's mad at the boy because he's ruining the scene. The other students are laughing and whispering. The teacher is looking at them angrily.

B2 A girl is sitting at her desk. She's studying for a test. Two of her friends are standing next to her and are trying to convince her to go to a party. The girl doesn't know what to do. She's afraid she'll do badly on the test if she doesn't study. Maybe she's afraid that her friends will like her less if she doesn't go with them.

Dialogues: Model answers

A1

A: What's the matter? Why are we losing?
B: I really don't know. But we can still win!
A: Why are we behind anyway? We've been training so hard for this match.
B: The other team is very good too, coach. And they're playing very aggressively.
A: Yes, I noticed. Anyway, just stay calm and don't get aggressive yourself. If you give your best, we can still win. Alright, let's go!

A2

A: Hi you two, are you OK?
B: Er … no, I'm having trouble with the last move. Could you do it again, please?
A: Yes, of course. Hey, you guys over there, stop laughing. That's not very nice! Look, I'll show you the moves again.
B: Thank you. I'll never remember all of them.
A: Don't worry. You just need some practice. And don't get nervous. Just have fun!

B1

B: I'm really sorry that I forgot my text. I was just so nervous. It was so embarrassing!
A: Don't worry. You can try again tomorrow.
B: Oh no! I can't go up on the stage again. Everybody was laughing at me.
A: Listen, nobody's perfect. Don't take the other students seriously. Why don't you look at your text again today and give it another try?
B: Well, OK.

B2

B: Come on, just come to the party. It'll be fun!
A: I don't know. There's a Maths test tomorrow and I want to get a good mark this time.
B: You're really smart, you don't have to study!
A: I don't understand this one exercise yet …
B: Everyone else from our class will be there!
A: Why don't you go to the party and give me one more hour to study? Then I'll come too!
B: OK, that sounds fair. See you later!

▲ **Role play:** A1: The team loses the game. What do the coach and the player say and/or do?
A2: One of the kids who was laughing fell while he/she was dancing at the show! One of the kids who had problems before was great. What do the kids say to each other?
B1: The actor and the actress talk after the show. What do they say to each other?
B2: The girl decided to go to the party and not study. What does she say to her mother/father?

Klett
Green Line 3
Vorschläge zur Leistungsmessung
ISBN: 978-3-12-834234-4

Unit 2

Warm up:
- What do you think Scotland and the Scottish people are like? What ideas do you have, and where do you have them from?
- Do you know what people from other countries think Germany and the German people are like? Give some examples. Where do you have them from?

Monologues: Model answers

A1 In this picture I can see a Scottish man and his wife. They both have red hair and they are wearing traditional Scottish clothes with a tartan pattern. They are standing in front of a shop. The man is looking at bagpipes; I think he'd like to buy them, but his wife looks angry because they are too expensive. There's a snack shop where you can buy haggis. The things about this picture that are "typically Scottish" are the traditional clothes, the bagpipes, the haggis and the fact that the woman doesn't want to spend money.

B1 In this picture I can see a German man and his wife at a train station. The man is wearing traditional German trousers and a hat, the woman is wearing a "Dirndl". There are stickers with "Ich liebe Fußball" and sports cars on the man's bag. The woman is eating a "Bratwurst". The man is afraid they will be late if she doesn't hurry. A board says that all trains are on time. The things that are "typically German" about the picture are the traditional German clothes, the "Bratwurst", the football and sports car stickers and the fact that the man wants to be on time.

A2 In this picture you can see a street full of people who want to vote in the Scottish referendum. There are lots of signs and balloons with "yes" and "no" on them and many Scottish flags. The people are all very excited. Many of them are wearing tartan kilts. A young woman is playing the bagpipes. The things about this picture that are "typically Scottish" are the Scottish kilts, the bagpipes and the Scottish flags.
I think the difference between the two pictures is that the second picture is a lot more positive. In my opinion, it shows how Scotland and the Scottish people really are better than the first picture.

B2 In this picture I can see cars on a German street and lots of happy people. Maybe Germany has won a big football match and the people are celebrating. They are hugging, cheering and waving German flags. The things that are "typically German" about the picture are the German cars, the flags and the fact that the Germans love football. The picture also shows that Germany is a multi-ethnic country. I think the first picture only shows things that people from other countries think about Germany, but there's more to Germany than this. The people in the second picture also look a lot happier. I think this is more what we Germans are really like.

Dialogues: Useful questions and phrases

- I'd like to go to/see … because …
- What do you think about …?
- How do you feel about …?
- Why don't we …?
- I think / In my opinion …

- I agree with you. / I disagree.
- I (don't) like this idea because …
- I (don't) think that's a good idea because …
- Yes, we should do that. / It would be better to …
- You've got a point but I'd prefer …

Dialogues:
Individuelle S-Antworten

▲ **Role play:** Partner A: Imagine you went to one of the places in the pictures. Partner B interviews you after you come back. Where did you go and what did you see? How did you like it? Did you have any exciting adventures?

Green Line 3
Vorschläge zur Leistungsmessung
ISBN: 978-3-12-834234-4

Unit 3

Warm up:
- Which period in time would you like to travel to? Why?
- Which historical figure would you like to meet? What would you ask him or her?

Monologues: Model answers

A Wow, I'm glad I made it back home safely! When I went back to the past, I landed in the middle of a Roman market. There were lots of people in Roman clothes. The women's dresses were so beautiful! I even saw a few Roman soldiers who were wearing helmets. The people were selling all kinds of different things, for example fruits and vegetables and jewellery. There were also some children who were playing. I was surprised that nobody had noticed me. I must have looked really strange in my modern clothes. I looked around and saw a man who was trying to steal a bag from a woman. What should I do? The Roman people would have noticed me if I had said something. But then the man looked around and saw that I was watching him. He was looking at me angrily. And of course he was very surprised to see me there. I don't really know what happened then … A moment later I was back in my room. What a trip!

B Nobody will ever believe what an adventure I had! When I got into the time machine, I planned to go to the Globe Theatre during Shakespeare's time, and it worked. It was amazing to feel what it was really like to be one of the people in the crowd back then! Our English teacher had shown us photos of the Globe, but I never imagined it to be so exciting! I tried to hide so that nobody would see me – because I would surely have been in trouble then! I was in the audience in front of the stage and watched the play. A man and a woman were acting a scene. I watched closely and noticed that the "woman" was really a man! I remembered that my teacher had told us that all the parts were acted by men at that time. It was so funny! While I was watching the "man", he suddenly looked at me too. He looked very shocked to see me and almost fell off the stage. "Oh no …," I thought, but before anything else could happen, I was back in my room. What a great adventure!

Dialogues: Model answers

Partner A/B (Set 1)

A: What am I doing here? What's going on?
B: Oh oh … Listen, something must have gone wrong …
A: Gone wrong? Who are you? Hey, didn't I see you at the market? Where's the market? And what are all these strange things here?
B: I think I took you back to this time with me.
A: What? This is a different time? Oooooh … are you a wizard?
B: No, I'm not a wizard. Listen, I'm really sorry about all this. I'll just send you back to your time. I think I need to fix the time machine …
A: I don't understand this. I want to go home!
B: Alright, I'll send you home. Just don't tell anybody in your time about this, OK?
A: Don't worry, nobody would believe me!

Partner A/B (Set 2)

A: What happened? Where am I?
B: Oh my God, are you …
A: I am the Queen of England! Who are you?
B: Wow, this is so cool!
A: Excuse me? This is not how you talk to a monarch. You are very rude!
B: I'm very sorry, I apologise.
A: Where have you brought me? Where is my lady-in-waiting? Help, help!
B: I don't know what has happened, but I don't want to hurt you. Don't be afraid.
A: What is this strange-looking thing over here?
B: That's my computer. I'll show you …
A: I don't know what magical trick this is, but I don't like it. I want you to bring me back now!
B: Oh, OK, I will. Sorry again! You just need to get into this machine …

▲ **Role play:** Partner A: You travelled back to Victorian/Celtic/Norman times and tell Partner B about it later. What did you see and do? Who did you talk to? How did you like this experience?

Klett
Green Line 3
Vorschläge zur Leistungsmessung
ISBN: 978-3-12-834234-4

Unit 4

Warm up:
- Where did you spend your last holiday? Did you like it?
- Have you ever had a funny/exciting/strange experience while you were on holiday?

Monologues: Model answers

A My father is worried that the weather might be bad all the time. He's also worried that there might be flight delays. He's afraid that he might forget his passport at home and that there will be trouble at passport control.
My mother is afraid of flying, so she's worried that there will be problems with the plane while it's up in the air. She's afraid that someone might steal her bag while she's swimming in the sea. She's also worried that the sun could burn her while she's at the beach and that she would be in pain then.

B My father is worried that a boat trip might be very boring because there are only old people and because there aren't any exciting activities to do. He's afraid that the boat might have an accident and sink. He also thinks that he might be seasick so that he wouldn't be able to enjoy the holiday any more.
My mother is afraid that our room on the boat might be really small and dark. She's worried that we might miss the departure of the boat when we take a day trip on land. She's also worried that a boat trip will be too expensive.

Dialogues: Useful questions and phrases

- What do you think about …?
- How do you feel about …?
- What's your opinion about …?
- I think …
- Why don't we …?
- I've got an idea. Can we …?
- Can we meet halfway?

- I (don't) think that's a good idea.
- I think you're forgetting that …
- I (don't) like this idea because …
- You've got a point but …
- I agree with you. / I disagree.
- I don't think we can do that.
- What about a compromise …

Dialogues: Model answer

A: Mum and Dad want us to decide where to go on our next summer holiday. I think that's great!
B: Yes, it is! I want to do something really exciting. What do you think about a trip to a big city?
A: Hm … Sorry, but I don't like this idea. I don't really like big cities. There are too many people there and it's always so loud. Why don't we go camping in the mountains? There'll be lots of beautiful nature and adventure. We could go hiking.
B: I don't think that's a good idea. A camping holiday is really boring! If we went to a big city, we could go shopping and see the sights. In the mountains there are just trees, lakes and animals!
A: I think you're forgetting that holidays in the mountains can be very exciting too. We could go canoeing or mountain climbing.
B: You've got a point, but I don't like camping. I'd rather stay in a nice hotel.
A: I don't think we can do that. A hotel in the city is really expensive and Mum and Dad probably don't want to spend too much money on a hotel.
B: Yes, I agree with you. But I still want to go shopping. I need some cool clothes and a new bag!
A: What about a compromise: We'll tell Mum and Dad we want to go to the mountains, but I'll go shopping with you before our holiday. We can go to the next biggest city by train. We'll have a fun day and I'll pay for lunch!
B: OK, that sounds fair. Let's do it!

▲ **Discussion:** Think about your next summer holidays and discuss what your perfect holiday would be like. Imagine that you can spend as much time and money there as you would like! Compare your ideas with your partner.

Green Line 3
Vorschläge zur Leistungsmessung
ISBN: 978-3-12-834234-4

Bewertung der Sprachkompetenz						
Kriterien/deren Erfüllung	voll	nahezu	im Wesentlichen	teilweise	kaum	nicht
inhaltlich richtig						
inhaltlich vollständig/ausführlich						
sprachlich verständlich						
sprachlich korrekt						
phonetisch korrekt						
intonatorisch korrekt						
adressaten-/ situationsgerecht						
selbstständig						

Green Line 3
Vorschläge zur Leistungsmessung
ISBN: 978-3-12-834234-4

Inhalt der Audio-CD

Hörverstehenstexte

Track	Unit	Test	Page	Title	Time
1	1	1	5	I need some advice!	01:50
2	1	2	6	Can we compromise?	01:36
3	2	1	17	Best of friends?	02:05
4	2	2	18	It always rains …	02:17
5	3	1	30	Who were they?	02:19
6	3	2	31	A class trip to the Globe	02:20
7	4	1	43	At the airport	02:53
8	4	2	44	"True" stories	02:19

Gesamtspielzeit: 17:42

Inhalt der CD-ROM

Filmsequenzen

Unit	Test	Page	Title	Time
2	14 Viewing	27	The Scottish referendum	01:24
3	17 Viewing	40	Shakespeare and the Globe	01:39

Gesamtspielzeit: 03:03

Außerdem finden Sie auf dieser CD-ROM:
- Materialien für Klassenarbeiten (inkl. Materialien für Viewing-Tests) und Lösungen
- alle *Speaking cards* und die dazugehörenden *Teacher's notes*
- alle Transkripte zu den Hörverstehenstexten und Filmsequenzen
- Förderempfehlungsmaterialien
- ein Bewertungsraster für die Speaking-Tests
- alle Hörverstehenstexte im mp3-Format

Systemvoraussetzungen der CD-ROM
- Windows 7/8/10
- Mac OS X 10.9/10.10/10.11/10.12
- 4 GB RAM
- DVD-ROM-Laufwerk
- Adobe Reader, enthält Audios (mp3), enthält Videos (mp4)

Sollten Sie Probleme mit dem vorliegenden Programm haben, finden Sie in den Dateien „Liesmich.txt" und „Lizenz.txt" unsere Kontaktdaten und weitere Hilfestellungen.